Dance *and* Grow

DANCE
and
GROW

Developmental Dance Activities for
Three- through Eight-Year-Olds

Betty Rowen, Ed. D.

A Dance Horizons Book
Princeton Book Company, Publishers
Pennington, NJ

A Dance Horizons Book
Princeton Book Company, Publishers
P.O. Box 57
Pennington, NJ 08534

Cover design by Frank Bridges
Interior design by Sue Bannon
Drawings by Suzette Armenteros and Humberto Lopez

Library of Congress Cataloging-in-Publication Data

Rowen, Betty.
   Dance and grow : developmental dance activities for three- through
eight-year-olds / Betty Rowen.
      p.   cm.
   "A Dance horizons book."
   Includes bibliographical references.
   ISBN 0-87127-196-6
   1. Dancing for children.   2. Movement education.   I. Title.
GV1799.R68   1994
372.6'6—dc20   93-46039

C O N T E N T S

F O R E W O R D

What greater gift do we have than our children? They are our dreams for the future and our hopes for a better world. The greatest gift we can give our children is to help them develop their creativity and realize their dreams. Every child has creativity, but not all children know how to access it. We must introduce, guide, and nuture these abilities.

Betty Rowen has been teaching children for her entire life. As a master teacher, she gives a child the ability to think creatively through movement. *Dance and Grow* gives you the tools to bring out a child's imagination. It will help children to think and be creative. It will lessen the fear to explore new ideas. It will also provide the technical tools to develop dance skills.

Through movement children can develop social and physical skills that will be helpful throughout their entire lives. At the New World School of the Arts I work with high-school and college students who are young dancers and. choreographers. I find some of my students more creative than others. The younger the student, the easier it is to bring out the creativity.

Start encouraging creativity early in life, for movement is a universal language that all children can speak, understand, and relate to. As a teacher or parent you can use the exercises, activities, movement qualities, and ideas in this book to help children reach their own creative potential. *Dance and Grow* is a wonderful book that will help children grow into mature, creative, fulfilled, and contributing adults. Hopefully, they will realize their later dreams through early movement.

Daniel Lewis
Dean of Dance
New World School of the Arts
Miami, Florida

P R E F A C E

This book applies basic dance principles to the teaching of dance to young children. Creative expression is essential in any class of children ages three through eight, thus the exercises and activities described in the book make use of imagery and involve a certain amount of freedom to explore the movement in each child's own way. Yet it is possible to integrate into each lesson some of the principles related to body alignment, muscle control, timing, spatial awareness, and quality of movement that will form the foundation for later study of ballet or modern dance.

Well-trained dancers do not always make this connection when teaching young children. They may include some dance technique in a manner similar to that taught to older children and adults. Games and play activity may be part of their lesson, but they are not always related to the development of dance skills. When children begin more formal lessons at age seven or eight, their previous experience in movement rarely has prepared them for the dance instruction they will receive in the dance studio.

Preschool teachers often use movement and dance as recreation or, possibly, to act out stories. Some now use movement daily to help children express ideas related to all areas of the curriculum. But rarely are classroom teachers aware of developmental sequences in dance education.

This book is addressed to both categories of teacher: those familiar with dance technique but who have little knowledge of child development, and those early childhood educators who may have little awareness of developmental sequences in movement and how they can be part of expressive forms of dance.

Dance and Grow begins with sequential exercises in axial and locomotor movements and shows their relation to later study. Following chapters discuss the basic elements of dance—rhythm, space, and quality of movement—and give activities to heighten awareness of these components. Themes for improvisation and simple group composition are also included. An appendix shows which exercises and activities in the text can be used to develop further understanding in the academic areas of language, number concept, social studies, science, art, and music.

This book will help studio teachers, physical educators, and nursery-level and primary-level teachers to enhance the value of movement in the classroom. Parents may also enjoy doing these exercises and activities at home with their preschoolers.

Dance and Grow is based on sound developmental principles, which are presented in a precise encapsulated format in the first chapter and applied to movement sequences throughout the book.

1

HOW MOVEMENT BEGINS

When Isadora Duncan was asked when she began dancing, she answered that it started in her mother's womb. To some extent, this is true for all of us. The fetus responds to loud rhythmic sound, often with strong kicks against the uterus wall. Perhaps it is owing to the nearness to the mother's heart that the developing fetus experiences and responds to rhythm. Certainly, this response occurs in newborns and throughout the first few months of life. Infants wave their arms excitedly when they hear music. They enjoy their mother's singing. They like to be rocked. Movement and rhythm are among the first forms of communication for the very young child.

Although newborns have very little control of their body, they can be seen to wave their arms and legs when excited. If one visits the nursery of a hospital, one can observe newborns with varying degrees of activity. Brazelton[1] has classified babies into active, moderate, and passive catagories. It is possible that these tendencies persist. Teachers observe differences in activity level and quality of movement in children in preschool settings and in movement classes. Awareness of these differences can help teachers to find movement activities suited to individual children.

Movement Patterns in the First Year of Life

By the time babies are ready to sit by themselves, they can be observed rocking back and forth rhythmically. A six-month-old at a laundromat with his mother was observed to rock precisely in time to the sound of the cycles of the washing machine. Here are movement patterns that are observed in children under the age of one:

Reaching and grasping: reflexes that are present at birth. Conscious control of arms and hands to reach for an object and grasp it begins at about four to six months. It is a major step in development because it signals not only conscious control but also the coordination of vision with movement of arm and hand.

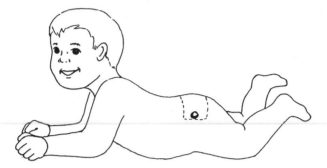

Movements in the First Year of Life

Head movements: among the first to develop in infants. They will turn their head to follow a moving object through a small arc of 90 degrees at one month. At four months, they enjoy propped-by-pillow sitting and holding the head up without support. Control of the head at this point allows babies to "track" an object for longer periods and in a wider arc. Also, at three-and-a-half or four months, they can raise their head close to 90 degrees from the horizontal while lying on their stomach. The head is then free to turn in a full arc so that they have full vision of their world.[2]

Turning over: first back to front in prone position, then front to back, begins at about three months. Once babies have learned to do this, they repeat the movement over and over in pure joy of achievement.

Hand movements: change at about six months. Babies can now use "pincer" motions with thumb in opposition to pointing finger to pick up small objects. They enjoy opening and closing the hands, and consciously reaching and grasping. They will pull on necklaces, grasp eyeglasses, and pick up small objects or lint from the carpet. They will also enjoy dropping things to exercise their control over objects (and people, who have to pick up these things).

Leg movements: also develop at about six months. Babies will extend their legs when they are held in a standing position and will attempt to support some of their weight.

Creeping: on hands and knees or on "all fours" can often occur with great alacrity at about eight months to one year. However, babies can pull themselves to standing position and can "cruise" sideways as they hold to a support. Falling down does not disturb them as they enjoy the change in levels and will try to climb back up again, sometimes falling down on purpose.

All of these activities are beginnings for later movement patterns. The hand movements of reaching and grasping are fun for the three-year-old as well as the three-week-old. Movements developing from this activity, such as stretching arms and hands and then closing in, are related to the infant's early explorations.

Activities on the floor—rolling over, changing perspective from back position to lying on the stomach, raising the head, and arching the back—are movements that can be developed into dance exercises, as we shall see in later chapters.

Changing levels—from creeping to standing and falling and getting up in various ways—can be incorporated into dance movements. Growing up from the ground, like a flower, makes children aware of levels, which, of course, are distinct areas for exploration by the dancer.

All movements that are close to the ground are enjoyable to young children. Awareness of the antecedent movement patterns of an infant can help the teacher of three- to six-year-olds to devise exercises relating to the familiar movements of this earlier stage.

Developing Sensorimotor Skills

Motor activity in the first years of life is important to total physical development, but it also enables babies to learn about the outside world. It is through movement that infants begin to coordinate their various sensations in order to learn about objects and things outside themselves.

Jean Piaget, the Swiss psychologist who has strongly influenced our thinking about the development of intelligence in children, has called this the "sensorimotor stage." Infants have only their own sensations. They must organize these into internal "schemata" or structures and must coordinate one sensory image with another to determine the nature of reality.

Suppose an infant is presented with a rattle. He can see it and hear it, but the

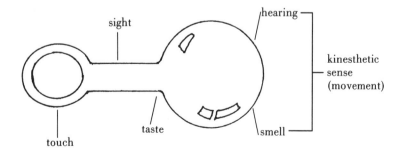

The Sensorimotor Stage Coordinates the Senses

eyes do not follow the sound because he does not realize that the visual image and the sound are related. By moving his hand until it makes contact with the rattle, he learns to know it as an outside object. All of his sensations become coordinated through this primary sensation, the kinesthetic sense.   The kinesthetic sense is an essential means of sensory experience throughout the first six years of life. It follows therefore, that movement should be involved in all kinds of learning.[3] As a teacher of dance to young children, even before I knew about Piaget's work, I was aware that the children I taught were learning many things in addition to the actual dance activities. Movement is a way of knowing.

Observing Preschool Children

Any teacher of young children needs to be a good observer. It would be a good idea to visit a hospital to see the neonates. Time samples will illustrate the variety of movements performed by them, and the differences in movement styles, degree of activity, and so forth exhibited by these babies who are only a few days old.

Observation of one-, two-, three-, and four-year-olds will reveal other startling differences. Visit playgrounds, beaches, parks, and airports. Focus on one child and observe him or her for two ten-minute sequences.* Full attention must be devoted to the task, and every aspect of the child's behavior should be noted. Make a small chart and put only overt behavior in the left-hand column. In the right-hand column, record your comments and interpretations of observed behavior.

Table 1

Time Sample for an Eleven-Month-Old

Time	Overt Behavior	Comments
10:33 a.m.	Creeps after ball that is under bench; reaches for it; pushes it; it rolls.	Moves quickly as if she knows where she is going.
10:35 a.m.	Creeps around leg of bench and goes under it, looks toward mother and smiles, leaves ball and creeps toward mother.	Is able to avoid bumping into leg of bench. After reaching ball, seems to lose interest in it. Seeks mother's approval.

(continued on following page)

*It is advisable to ask parents' permission before observing any child.

Table 1

Time Sample for an Eleven-Month-Old
(continued)

Time	Overt Behavior	Comments
10:36 a.m.	Reaches for edge of bench, uses it to help herself up, falls down, gets back again.	Can stand when holding onto something. Enjoys falling and getting up.
10:37 a.m.	Mother tells her to dance. Big smile, bounces up and down, standing and holding onto bench. Laughing.	Understands mother's request and follows directions. Enjoys rhythmic activity.
10:38 a.m.	Grabs for ball again, this time firmly with both hands. Throws ball.	Reaching, grasping, throwing skills have developed.

From Betty Rowen, *The Children We See* (New York: Holt, Rinehart and Winston, 1973), p. 119.

Although teachers of dance may never be involved with an eleven-month-old, the skills and interests of one- to three-year-old babies reveal a great deal that is related to teaching preschoolers.

The baby in the Time Sample was able to creep, which two-, three-, and four-year-olds still enjoy doing. Changing levels, that is, falling down and getting up, was great fun for this eleven-month-old, as it is for most children in the very early years. Bouncing in time to music while standing and holding on to something is done by most one-year-olds. Younger babies have been observed bouncing to music while seated. Two- and three-year-olds may do a little galloping step as well as bouncing in place. Thus, it is evident that "dancing" begins very early.

The Time Sample is very helpful in letting teachers know at what level children are functioning. It is strongly recommended that readers follow the illustration of a Time Sample and do some for themselves. Careful analysis of these observations will enable an assessment of the developmental level at which a child is operating. This will be useful in placing the child in the best group for him, and will also help teachers to select appropriate activities and dance exercises.

Motor Characteristics of One- Through Eight-Year-Olds

One-year-olds: The motor activities of children in the first year of life and a characteristic Time Sample of an eleven-month-old have been presented.

Children in the second year of life (twelve through twenty-three months) are physically very active. They have become two-legged creatures and prefer the upright position. As a matter of fact, they will practice standing up every chance they get. Very often children at this age will not remain lying down when put to bed, but will continuously stand up, holding on to the crib, until they finally fall down from exhaustion.

This period is often referred to as the "toddler" stage, for the characteristic walk is with feet far apart and head plus upper portion of the trunk thrust forward. At a year and a half (eighteen months), children's steps are longer, the walk width is reduced, and they can now walk sideways and backwards. They love to climb. They can creep up steps, but probably go down backwards or by sitting bumps.

Perhaps the outstanding achievement at this age is running. Balance is improved and they can even stand on one foot if given support. All of this activity should be encouraged but needs to be carefully supervised. One- to three-year-olds usually do not know caution, and will try anything.

Two- to three-year-olds: During the period from two to three years, walking becomes highly automatized. Two-year-olds can walk a straight line without the

TABLE 2

Motor Development of Children from Birth to Three Years

A. PREREQUISITE INFORMATION   1. MOTOR DEVELOPMENT

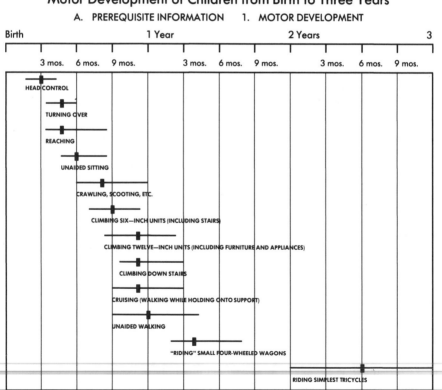

From Burton L. White, *The First Three Years of Life* (Englewood Cliffs, NJ: Prentice Hall, 1975), p. 219.

wide stance of the toddler. They can run and gallop and take short running steps on their toes. They can jump several inches off the floor.

Rocking is a favorite activity. Children this age love to be rocked by an adult; they love rocking horses and other rocking toys and learn to propel themselves quite well. They will rock from side to side when they hear music, and can keep time by waving arms and hands.

Table 2 (see page 6) describes motor development for children from birth to three years.

Three-year-olds:[4] At age three, walking has become more uniform in length, width, and speed of step. For the first time, we can observe heel-toe progression, instead of the flatfoot walk of the toddler. Three-year-olds can balance their weight momentarily on the toes and take short steps in this manner. They can run easily and smoothly with moderate control of speed. They use alternate feet in ascending and descending stairs. This increase in coordination tells us that three-year-olds can engage in dance exercises. This is one of the reasons we have chosen this age as the beginning for teaching dance.

Another important factor is that three-year-olds can follow directions. They are much more willing to please adults than are two-year-olds, and are eager to show how grown-up they are by performing simple routines on their own, such as brushing teeth. Three-year-olds are great imitators, and can learn simple motions (touching "head, shoulders, knees, and toes") by copying an adult's actions. Their interest span is short, however, and imitative activity needs to be followed by free movements and resting periods. This is a good time to begin story dramatization and finger plays.

Four-year-olds: By the age of four, children walk with long, swinging steps in an adult style. Their arms swing in opposition to the feet; they swing in opposition when they skip, an activity that most children can handle well at this stage.

As a matter of fact, all parts of the body are better coordinated. They can follow directions using arm patterns along with leg movements and can change those patterns when instructed. They take great pleasure in doing stunts, such as whirling, swinging, and somersaulting. They balance well on the toes, and can jump higher and in different directions.

All of these new skills can be incorporated into dance activities. Four-year-olds love to move and find it hard to sit still for very long. This heightened activity can be difficult to deal with, and the teacher needs to have signals (such as *Freeze!)* to halt the activity and to get control.

Four-year-olds are less interested in pleasing adults than are "three's." Their main concern seems to be social interaction with peers. They are competitive, and like to see "who can jump higher" or "who can run faster." This is a good time for "follow-the-leader" and "Simon says" types of games, where dance motions can be used and simple patterns established.

Five-year-olds: Five-year-olds have mastered most of the activities performed at earlier ages, but now can do them with ease, grace, and economy of movement. Their keen sense of balance and versatility in the use of hands and feet show that they are ready for the more complex activities of later childhood. "Five's" can walk on their toes without touching heels to the floor. They can take longer steps, extending runs into leaps and varying types of walking. They can skip or march in time to music, and can play rhythm instruments to a set rhythm.

Temperamentally, "five's" are well suited to a learning situation. This is a leveling-off period. Children are less assertive and more willing to follow rules of behavior. They will "take turns," wait in line, and generally seem to have a better understanding of social behavior.

This is a time when circle games and simple folk dances, such as "Skip to My Lou," can be taught. It is also a time when children can work in small groups, accompanying each other on rhythm instruments or creating simple group improvisations.

Six-year-olds: Six-year-olds are interested in competence. Along with their new status as school-age children who are required to read and write, they consider their personal abilities a reflection of individual worth. They ask themselves, "Can I do these things well?"

By six, individual differences emerge more sharply. Well-coordinated children can catch and throw a ball and can excel on the playground. For some, this skill can build self-esteem, especially where reading skills may be slow in developing. There are also more marked differences between boys and girls. Small-muscle coordination seems to develop faster in girls. Boys become interested in sports and try to acquire skills that will help them achieve success in this area.

Movement activities for boys can be related to this interest. Images of basketball players can motivate boys to jump, pivot, and swing arms. Pairing off, they can react to their partners' movements as if guarding a basketball player. Girls are likely to want to become ballerinas. Although society seems to encourage these sex distinctions, opportunities to experience all types of movement should be available and encouraged for boys and girls alike. This is a time when role-playing stories like "Cinderella" or "Hansel and Gretel" can be used to develop dance movements for both sexes.

Seven-year-olds: Seven-year-olds are still strongly interested in competence. But now a new element of competition seems to prevail. It is likely that seven-year-olds will try to outdo each other in whatever activity they pursue. Girls, particularly, seek the teacher's approval and love to tattle on others who may not be doing as well.

Although competition can be useful in learning situations, it should not be emphasized to the detriment of any class member. This is a time when small group activity can be used for improvisations or "team" performances. Groups should be balanced so that some good performers are on each "team" and those with creative ideas for improvisation are similarly well distributed among the groups.

Eight-year-olds: Interest in skill development is at its height at this age. Children learn to skate, to dive and swim, to jump rope, to play ball. All of these things are special accomplishments that help to develop a self-concept and to establish prestige in peer groups.

In dance class, girls want to wear tutus and toe shoes. They should be discouraged from beginning toe dancing until their feet are strong enough and they have performed the basic ballet positions on demi-pointe (half-toes). While previously these same children enjoyed making up their own dances, they now prefer to learn routines.

Creativity is on the wane at this age. Children ask for directions and are less willing to use their own judgment. Perhaps this is owing to the treatment children are receiving in school, where conformity is often expected of them. It is important that opportunities for creativity be continued with "routines" developing from children's own combination of movement.

Good Teaching Practices for Three- Through Eight-Year-Olds

Good teaching practices must be based on knowledge of the developmental level at which the children are operating. The brief summaries of the characteristics of age groups from one through eight may be used as guidelines, but children differ individually. A well-coordinated four-year-old may be able to work along with "five's" or "sixes," while a five-year-old whose physical development is slow will do better in a class with younger children. Observation is an important tool for teachers.

Skipping is a good indication of physical readiness. Children who can skip, swinging arms in alternation to leg movements, show maturity in physical development. Skipping requires being able to hop off the ground and return to the same foot, thus exhibiting balancing skills. Alternating arms shows overall coordination of different body parts.

It is important for teachers to maintain a warm, accepting attitude toward the young children in their class. Lots of praise makes children feel good about themselves and what they are doing. The rigid manner of a formal ballet teacher is not suitable in the classes we are describing. Although corrections may be made to improve body alignment, arm positions, and so forth, variation from the exercise being taught should be accepted. For example, the teacher might say, *I like your arm swings, but can you also try to bend your knees a little as you go down and up?*
Imagery is very important in teaching young children. As a matter of fact, it should be the starting place for presenting dance exercises. Floor exercises may be demonstrated by the teacher, but can be followed up immediately with the suggestion of *Let's all be sailboats!* or *Can you be a cat like this?* Sometimes children make up their own images. For example, when a teacher asked her class to close in and open up as a stretching exercise, one child commented, "That is like my mother's bridge chairs. They fold and open." After that, the exercise was called "folding chairs" by the class.

Improvisations based on poems or stories are really extensions of images. Before telling the story of "The Little Rocking Horse" (see p. 85), the teacher may ask, *Have you ever been on a rocking horse? Show me how it rocks.* Imagery is used throughout the story as children improvise their movements of race horses, policemen's horses, or circus horses.

Whenever images are used the teacher should be sure that references are understood by everyone in the class. Pictures or small models of sailboats can be brought in, and the mast identified. A rocking horse, or a small replica of one (Christmas tree ornaments often include one of these), can be used to demonstrate rocking movement. Chairs that fold and open are available in most schools.

Improvisation should be part of every class for young children. After a particular movement has been presented, good questions to ask might be *Can you do it another way?* or *How many ways can you swing?* Children can make up their own patterns of movement by combining walks and jumps or runs and leaps. This may begin with a rhythmic pattern, such as playing the rhythm of children's names and then asking them to move to that rhythm (see p. 49–51). Or, in teaching a step coming across the floor, the children may be asked to add something (a turn, jump, etc.) to the step they have just been practicing.

Flexibility on the teacher's part must be maintained throughout the class. If the children are having a hard time learning a step, it might be better to stop, move to something familiar, and save the difficult step for another time. The amount of time spent on floor exercises or movements in space must be regulated by the mood of the class (see class organization below). Active movements should alternate with quiet movements. When children get too wild, the teacher needs to know how to slow them up or get them to rest.

Control should never be administered harshly. A signal established at the beginning of the class can be used to get the attention of the children. If the teacher uses a drum, then holding her stick in the air might mean the children need to be quiet and listen for directions.

Piano chords can be used similarly. Saying *Freeze!* or *Be a statue* might get the same result. Rarely, a child may be asked to sit down and wait until he can be quiet, before dancing again. The waiting period should be short, and the child should be invited to join the group as soon as possible.

If a child does not want to participate, there are ways to get her started. A role in a story dramatization that requires little activity might help: *Can you be the king's attendant for a while, and just stay with him during the dance?* If rhythm instruments are used, a child might be asked to keep time for a dancer, thus involving the nonparticipant while he is sitting on the sidelines.

Class organization should also be flexible. Younger children ("three's" and "four's") should have only a half hour of dance activity, increasing as interest level improves. The sequence of activities is also a matter of the teacher's discretion. The younger the group, the more frequently the activity must change. Here are some suggestions for sequencing:

Floor exercises: stretches, leg lifts, etc.	5 minutes
Standing exercises: swings, stretches, pliés	5 minutes
Activities in circle or across the floor	5 minutes
Rest (story may be told at this time)	15 minutes
Story improvisations	Remainder of class

Warm-ups of some kind should precede leaps or jumps, and exercises (with imagery) should precede improvisations. A coordinating theme might be used for some lessons, so that exercises prepare the class for the improvisational theme.

Notes

1. T. Berry Brazelton, *Infants and Mothers: Differences in Development* (New York: Dell, 1969).
2. Burton L. White, *The First Three Years of Life* (Englewood Cliffs, NJ: Prentice Hall, 1975), p. 48.
3. See Betty Rowen, *Learning Through Movement*. 2d ed. (New York: Teachers College Press, Columbia University, 1982).
4. An exemplary table of the characteristics and needs of three- through six-year-olds, with suggestions for classroom activity, can be found in Diane Lynch Fraser, *Playdancing: Discovering and Developing Creativity in Young Children* (Pennington, NJ: Princeton Book Company, Publishers, 1991), pp. 12–16.

2

AXIAL DEVELOPMENTAL MOVEMENT SEQUENCES

M ovement can be divided into two categories. There are those movements that are done staying in one place, and those that transport the body from one place to another. Movements that do not take us from place to place are called "axial" movements. They involve the trunk, legs, arms, and head in actions such as bending, stretching, and swinging.

These nonlocomotor exercises form much of the basis for systems of adult dance techniques. However, the basic elements can be presented to young children if imagery and games are part of the presentation.

Various kinds of axial and locomotor movements are defined in Chapters 2 and 3, respectively. Step-by-step exercises are described with accompanying imagery and the relation of each exercise to dance technique.

Body Alignment

Alignment in ballet means essentially good posture [1]; that is, the various body parts—head, shoulders, arms, ribs, hips, legs, feet—are in correct relative position with each other. Bad posture can result in a slump [2], with rounded shoulders and droopy head, or a sway [3] with pelvis released backward causing a hollow look to the lower back. These distortions in alignment are detrimental enough to an ordinary body, but they can be positively hazardous for the ballet student.[1]

It is never too soon to make the young child aware of good posture. Parents tell their children to "stand up straight," but the positions of the head, neck shoulders, and back are not described. In dance class, teachers can offer exercises that

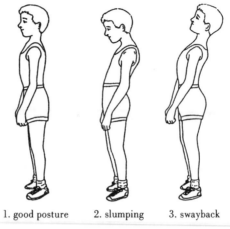

1. good posture   2. slumping   3. swayback

Body Alignment

create good body alignment, while still "playing games" with three- through eight-year-olds.

Young children can be made aware of their body positions without use of any technical language. Only the teacher need know the relation to ballet or modern dance technique that can be found in the simple exercises described below.

✿ E X E R C I S E 1

Starting position: Seated on the floor with bottoms of the feet together and knees straightened to the side and down as far as possible. Hands should rest on the ankles.

Step 1: In this position, put the head to the toes, rounding the back and keeping the face down.

Step 2: Slowly sit up, starting at the base of the spine and putting one vertebra (part of the spine) on top of the other. The head comes up last.

Step 3: Straighten the spine, keeping the neck long, the shoulders down, and the head looking straight forward. Holding the ankles firmly helps to keep the shoulders down.

Repeat, putting head to toes and straightening.

Imagery: In Step 1, *put your feet together as if you were clapping feet.* In Step 3, the teacher may go around to each student to see if there are any bumps in the back. If the back is not straight, a gentle touch on the rounded portion will make the child aware of the back position. *Get the bump out of your back.* In this straight-back position, children may rock from one side to the other. *You are a sailboat and the mast down the center must be kept straight as you rock.* Thereafter, the children may call this exercise "sailboats."

Relation to dance technique: The same exercise is performed in many adult dance classes, usually as a beginning warm-up. In a more advanced version, the

Preparation for "Sailboats"

move to put head to toes is done as a contraction, beginning with a tightening of the stomach muscles, then the back and head following this initial impulse. Straightening the back can begin with the lower spine, before coming to a vertical sitting position. This version can be introduced to five- and six-year-olds only after they have become familiar with correct body alignment, as described above.

❀ E X E R C I S E 2

Starting position: On the knees, hands on floor, body raised off the floor.
Step 1 (beginning movement): Round the back, pulling up in the middle into a hump, with the head hanging down.
Step 2: Straighten the back so it is flat, head in a straight line with the back.
Step 3: Arch the back so that it curves downward. Head comes up to look ahead.
Repeat, rounding, flattening, and arching the back.

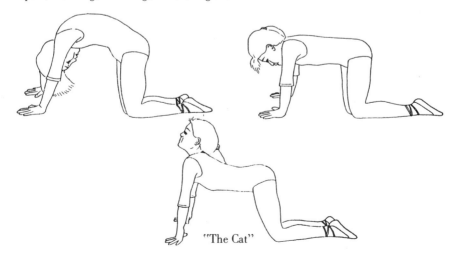

"The Cat"

Imagery: *You are an angry cat* (possibly at Halloween) *rounding and arching your back. You may want to say "Meow" as you arch your back.* Make the children keep "meowing" down to a minimum—only as they arch the back.
Relation to dance technique: Children become aware of back positions. A hollow look, as in the arched position, is not desirable in most ballet movements and may lead to lordosis (swayback). However, the difference between rounded, straight, and arched back can be understood only by experiencing these three positions.
See also Appendix: Exercises, Activities, and Themes That Can Be Used to Enhance Learning in Academic Areas, Exploring Science, p. 101.

❀ E X E R C I S E 3

Starting position: Stand with "good posture," eyes straight ahead, shoulders down, feet parallel, knees straight but not "locked" (overextended).
Step 1: Drop forward from the waist, head down, arms to the floor in relaxed position.
Step 2: Come up to standing position slowly, putting one vertebra on top of the other until standing position is reached. Head comes up last.
Step 3: Raise arms slowly to the side and up overhead. Stretch higher, making sure that shoulders are down, neck straight, eyes looking forward as stretch is executed.
Step 4: Drop down suddenly to position in Step 1. A percussive *and-Drop* from the overhead stretch adds an element of surprise and fun to the exercise.
Repeat Steps 2−4.

"The Marionette"

Imagery: *You are a marionette and the strings are pulling you to an upright position. When you drop down, the puppeteer has let go of the strings.* Step 4 may be done slowly, in which case the children might be directed to melt like a snowman.

Relation to dance technique: Again, the students are being made aware of body alignment as they place one vertebra on top of the other, coming to an overhead stretched position. There is also a beginning awareness of stretch and release (relaxed) positions. When overhead stretch is executed, the body may tighten, pulling buttocks in and tightening stomach muscles. In dropping down, a release is experienced and body should hang loose in total relaxation.

See also Appendix: Exercises, Activities, and Themes That Can Be Used to Enhance Learning in Academic Areas, Exploring Science, p. 101.

Swings

A swing is a movement of a part of the body in an arc or circle around a stationary center. The swinging part of the body is released to the force of gravity and is carried up to the opposite side of the arc as far as the compelling power of the drop will carry it. Then it falls back into the gravity pull again.

Swinging is a very natural movement for young children. On the playground, their arms swing as they walk, skip, or run. Standing still is hard for them; frequently they swing their arms around their body as they wait in line with their class. All of us swing our arms as we walk briskly, and the swing adds vigor to the movement.

So, it follows that swinging movements should be an early and consistent part of the dance curriculum. From simple swings of body parts to more involved movements to accompany foot patterns, jumps, or falls, the swing is an essential part of the dance vocabulary for all dancers.

✿ E X E R C I S E 1

Starting position: Swinging can develop out of Exercise 3 of Body Alignment (p. 16).

From the overhead stretch in the standing position, the direction *and-Drop* can become *Drop down and swing.*

Step 1: The impetus of the drop allows the arms to swing, brushing the floor and continuing behind the body. The whole body, as well as the arms, should swing from the waist, arms relaxed as they follow the arc of the swing.

Step 2: The swing continues as the arms swing back up to the overhead position. Movement continues to drop down and swing back in 3/4 time. *(And-Drop-2-3 and-Up-2-3.)*

Imagery: It is important that the swing has the quality of a fall, and that the arms drop, rather than being placed, in the arc movement. The teacher may help by holding up one arm, directing that it be made loose *(like a rag doll)* and

Swinging

letting it go so that it drops naturally by the pull of gravity.

There are many dramatic images that come to mind involving swinging. Some of them are elephants' trunks, bears, the man on the flying trapeze, pendulums, golf swings. Of course, the obvious image is of a swing on the playground.

Various parts of the body can swing, as the teacher suggests, *Make your arms be a swing ... make your whole body swing.* And finally, *Swing any way you want to—make up your own kind of swing.* Some lovely movements may result from these improvisations. The teacher may select one or two swinging patterns to be demonstrated and the class may try different ones.

Robert Louis Stevenson's poem "The Swing" can be recited to accompany the swings. The rhythm of the poem follows exactly the swinging rhythm of the movements. A simple structure can be given to group improvisations by setting different types of swings to different parts of the poem. For example:

> *How do you like to go up in a swing,*
> *Up in the air so blue?*
> *Oh, I do think it the pleasantest thing*
> *Ever a child can do.*

Movement here can be side-to-side swings, shifting weight from one foot to the other, or any other movement selected from earlier improvisations.

> *Up in the air and over the wall,*
> *Till I can see so wide,*
> *Rivers and trees and cattle and all*
> *Over the countryside—*

Movements might be forward and back swings, with a hop on the forward foot as the arms swing up high.

> *Till I look down on the garden green,*
> *Down on the roof so brown—*
> *Up in the air I go flying again,*
> *Up in the air and down!*

Low swings around the body are suggested for the first part of this stanza, with a repeat of the high swing with a hop at the end.

Relation to dance technique: Coordinating body parts in swinging movement calls forth a sense of balance when the weight shifts, as in a side-to-side swing. Swinging movements can change in quality, creating dances that are soft and lyrical (perhaps to Chopin waltzes) or vigorous and percussive (as in fighting movements). It would be hard to find a piece of choreography that does not use swinging movements in some part of the composition.

See also Appendix: Exercises, Activities, and Themes That Can Be Used to Enhance Learning in Academic Areas, Language Development, p. 96.

❀ E X E R C I S E 2

Starting position: Stand with legs apart about one foot and feet straight ahead. Body is relaxed, arms and hands loose at the sides.

Step 1: Shift body weight from one foot to another. Arms will begin to swing across the body. Placing weight on left foot, right arm will cross in front of body and left arm will circle behind body. As weight changes, arms reverse position.

Step 2: Increase force, so that arms are swinging in a horizontal arc around the body. As weight-shifting increases in strength, the knee bends on the side receiving the weight.

Step 3: On the third swing, children may pivot in a circle, continuing the arm swing. The count is *swing-2-3, swing-2-3, spin around-and-swing-2-3.*

The last swing is a continuation of the movement that takes the body into the pivot. The foot pattern in the swing need not be emphasized. Some children take little steps as they turn in a circle; others may pivot on the toes of one foot.

Imagery: Tops spinning, gears of a machine, basketball players.

Relation to dance technique: Shifting weight leading to a turn is used in many dance forms. Arms swinging help the dancer to turn, as in ballet piqué turns.

Stretch—Bend

Stretching and bending usually go together. Stretching occurs whenever there is a full extension of any part of the body in any possible direction. Bending describes a type of movement in which two adjacent sections of the body are brought closer together. There should be some kind of stretching and bending as warm-up at the beginning of every class.

❀ E X E R C I S E 1

Starting position: Standing with "good posture," feet parallel and slightly apart, eyes forward, arms overhead.

Step 1: Reach slowly with one arm toward the ceiling. *(Can you make that arm longer than the other?)*

Step 2: Release the tension in that arm and slowly stretch toward the ceiling with the other arm.

Step 3: Bring arms to the side, raised to shoulder height. Reach slowly with one arm toward the wall.

Step 4: Return to center and reach slowly with the other arm toward the opposite wall.

Imagery: All movements are sustained, without bounces or sharp angles. *A helium balloon, as in the Thanksgiving Day Parade, is lifting your arm higher as you try to hold on to it. You are reaching for something high up on a tree, or on a shelf on the wall (but you cannot step sidewards).*

Relation to dance technique: Muscles must be stretched slowly to warm up for any later activity.

❀ E X E R C I S E 2

Starting position: Sit on the floor, knees bent and brought to chest, arms holding knees, head down. (*You are a ball.*)

How Many Ways Can You Stretch?

Step 1: Open up slowly, reaching out with arms and legs until legs are extended out on the floor, knees straight, toes pointed, head up, neck straight, shoulders down. (*Don't lose your neck!*)
Step 2: Return to starting position. Repeat activity in a fast, percussive movement. (*and-Stretch! and-Close in!*)
Imagery: Can be done on the knees. *You are a turtle coming in and out of his shell. What else closes and opens?*
Relation to dance technique: Many ballet movements require opening up from a center position. "Closing in" can develop into contractions if emphasis is placed on using the stomach muscles as a starting impulse for closing.

EXERCISE 3
"How Many Ways Can You Stretch?"

Starting position: May be any position child chooses.
Step 1: Reach as far as possible in any direction.
Step 2: Hold position (*like statues*). Teacher looks for interesting positions. May suggest improvements. (*Straighten this knee* or *Make your neck long.*)
Step 3: Pull into the middle and fold up in any position.
Step 4: Repeat, trying to find another stretch position.
Imagery: Statues, funny clowns, turtles, snails, waking up in the morning. An imaginary elastic band can be placed between two parts of the body (e.g. elbow and knee). *How far can the elastic stretch? Now make it snap back. Place it between two other body parts.*
Relation to dance techniques: Students create their own shapes in space. They become aware of patterns that are interesting. They make their own contributions to class exercise, perhaps when one student is selected to demonstrate his movement (statue). They may play "follow the leader," thus beginning to relate to each other in group formations.

EXERCISE 4
Knee Bends (Pliés)

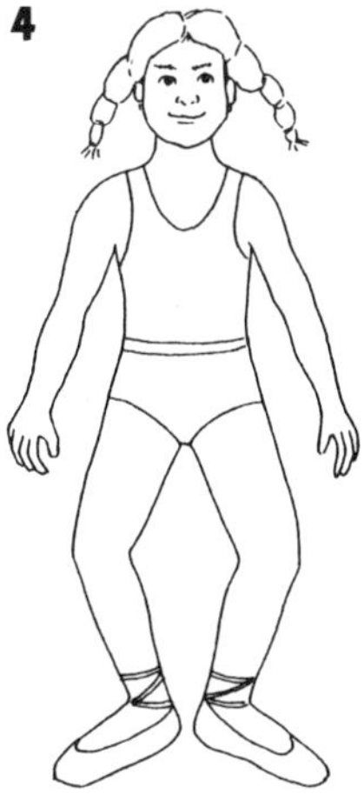

Starting position: Stand with heels touching and toes apart (first position).
Step 1: Bend knees, opening them over the toes, keeping back straight and tall.
Do not lift heels off the floor.
Step 2: Stretch up slowly, closing knees tightly and straightening the legs.
Repeat, at first going down slightly (demi-plié), later going down to the floor
(grand plié). Also try with legs apart and toes turned out (second position).
Imagery: Knees out *like you are opening a window,* back straight as you go
down *like in a very narrow elevator shaft—you cannot lean forward or backward.*
Relation to dance technique: Demi-plié is very important because all
springing steps, leaps, and jumps begin and end with it.

Body Isolation Movements

In isolation movements, one part of the body is moved at a time, thus
developing body awareness. This is not easy for young children, and it takes
concentration, but it is fun. In addition to learning to control one part of the
body at a time, the children are also learning the names of body parts and what
they can do.

Various Body Parts

❀ **E X E R C I S E**

Starting position: Sit on the floor, legs crossed, arms at sides.
Step 1: Bounce hands up and down, moving from the wrist. (*You are bouncing
a ball. Now can you make it bounce off the side walls? Off the ceiling?*) Bounce
hands in different directions. A drum, or some strongly rhythmic music, such as
African music or soft rock, can be used for accompaniment. It is helpful if the
tempo and volume accelerate as the exercise continues.
Step 2: Bounce shoulders in different directions, first up and down. (*You are
saying "I don't know."*) Now push shoulders forward and back.
Step 3: Make head bounce (*You are saying "Yes."*) Then bounce head to one
side—to the other side—to the back.
Step 4: Make elbows bounce. (*Your elbows are bouncing the ball.*) Bounce elbows
in different directions.
Step 5: Make elbows lead and come to a standing position. Move around, letting
elbows lead.
Step 6: Make hips bounce in different directions. Let hips lead in movements
around the room.
Step 7: Move more slowly and return to sitting position. (*Keep one part of you
bouncing! Bounce your knees. Now bounce your buttocks as you sit. Now elbows.
Now shoulders. Now hands. Make the bounces smaller, but keep bouncing until the
music stops.*)
Imagery: Various parts of the body are used to bounce an imaginary ball. Later,

children can do improvisations, giving themes to head dances, hand dances, and so forth.

Relation to dance technique: Every dancer must be able to isolate movement, sometimes moving only one part of the body, for accent or to enhance meaning. *See also* Appendix: Exercises, Activities, and Themes That Can Be Used to Enhance Learning in Academic Areas, Social Learning, p. 96.

Feet

❀ E X E R C I S E 1

Starting position: Sit on the floor, legs extended forward, feet together.
Step 1: Point toes forward, keeping heels on the floor, knees straight.
Step 2: Point toes back, heels forward, bending ankles as far as they can go without bending knees.
Repeat, pointing toes, then heels. (*Your toes are saying "Hello" to me.*)

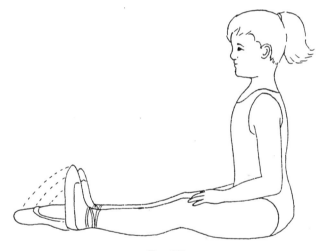

Feet Warmup

❀ E X E R C I S E 2

Starting position: Stand, feet slightly apart and parallel.
Step 1: Point one foot to the front, weight on opposite foot. Pull foot back, heels on floor, weight on both feet.
Repeat on other side, and alternate. Try same exercise to the side, making sure that knee points to ceiling.
Step 2: Point toe to the front. Touch lightly to floor and raise off floor.
Repeat several times. Do same movement on opposite foot, also to the side.
Return to standing position with weight on both feet between each change.
Imagery: In Exercise 1, the toes are saying "Hello" to someone seated opposite

(usually the teacher). In Exercise 2, the children can pretend they are wading in water: *The water is too cold. Now lift up your toe. Now try touching the water again lightly.*

Relation to dance technique: The ankles and feet are being used to stretch, or point, the toes. All elevation is dependent on the ability to stretch and flex the ankles and feet. Exercise 2 is preparation for ballet "petit battement."

Leg Lift (Battement)

Hands

❀ E X E R C I S E 1

Starting position: Sit on the floor, legs crossed. Begin with both hands clenched.

Step 1: Spread both hands with palms facing forward.

Step 2: Return to clenched position.

Repeat.

Step 3: Play hand game to this poem.

> *Open, shut them, open, shut them*
> *Give a little clap*
> *Open, shut them, open, shut them*
> *Put them in your lap.*
>
> *Creep them, creep them, creep them, creep them*
> *Way up to your chin*
> *Open up your little mouth*
> *But do not put them in!*

On the second verse, both hands should be used, fingers walking up the body toward the mouth. On the last line, the hands are quickly withdrawn and placed behind the back.

See also Appendix: Exercises, Activities, and Themes That Can Be Used to Enhance Learning in Academic Areas, Language Development, p. 96.

❀ E X E R C I S E 2

Step 1: From clenched hand position, raise one finger at a time and return to clenched fist after all have been raised. Play "This little piggie went to market." Begin with thumb, ending with "pinkie" on "All the way home," return to fist position.

See also Appendix: Exercises, Activities, and Themes That Can Be Used to Enhance Learning in Academic Areas, Number Concepts, p. 98.

❀ E X E R C I S E 3

Step 1: To find the correct position for relaxed and ballet hands, hold arms to the sides (second position) with hands clenched into fists. Slowly release the tension in the hands and let them relax. Keep wrists extended. (*Your hands are resting on the air.*)

❀ E X E R C I S E 4

Step 1: Keeping hands relaxed, rotate them from the wrists, making a circle. Change directions.

Step 2: Draw a figure-eight in the air, letting hands lead as they rotate: thumb leads as the hands rotate in, palms down; rotate wrist; thumb leads out with palms up. Make movement bigger, involving arms.

Imagery: In addition to the hand games above, older groups might try imitating the hand movements of Oriental dancers (show pictures). Other suggestions might be sign language or policemen directing traffic. Improvise to "He's got the whole world in his hands."

Relation to dance technique: Flexibility of wrists and fingers is essential for all dance. This flexibility carries over into use of the hands in raising and lowering the arms in "port de bras." Expressive hands are an important part of dance.

See also Appendix: Exercises, Activities, and Themes That Can Be Used to Enhance Learning in Academic Areas, Number Concepts, p. 98.

Arms

❀ E X E R C I S E 1

Step 1: Walking in a circle, raise arms to the side to shoulder height. Elbows and wrists should be relaxed. Hands should be in line with arms, fingers relaxed but not drooping.

Step 2: Continue walking in a circle, lower arms to sides, wrists leading.

Step 3: Increase tempo to light running steps, but continue arm movements at same slow pace (if using a waltz accompaniment, take six counts to raise arms and six to lower, while running six steps for each).

Step 4: Repeat walk with arms coming forward and back. Wrists lead on forward movement, but return to position in line with arms when returning to open (second) position.

Imagery: Steps 1, 2, and 3 resemble birds flying. Step 4 resembles butterflies, whose wings close and open over the body rather than at the side of the body. Suitable music for these images can easily be found, and/or stories can be developed.

See also Appendix: Exercises, Activities, and Themes That Can Be Used to Enhance Learning in Academic Areas, Exploring Science, p. 101.

❀ E X E R C I S E 2

Step 1: Standing with good posture, feet slightly turned out, raise arms overhead slightly in front of head. (*Make a picture frame*).

Step 2: Lower arms to the sides until in line with shoulders.

Step 3: Continue to lower arms, but rotate wrists so palms are facing downward.

Step 4: Return arms to side.

Repeat.

Imagery: Since this is a shortened port de bras, which is done in ballet classes, children can think of themselves as "ballet dancers." Later, this arm movement can be combined with a ballet walk (see Step 7 of Walks, p. 30).

Legs

❀ E X E R C I S E 1

Step 1: Lying on back on the floor, raise one leg with toes pointed, knees straight. Lower leg to floor. Do this with the other leg. Alternate legs.

Step 2: Lying on back on the floor, raise one knee to chest, then straighten leg, pointing toe to the ceiling. Lower straightened leg to floor. Do same movement with other leg. Set tempo to a comfortable rate for children. (*Bend—and Straighten—and Down.*)

❀ E X E R C I S E 2

Step 1: Lying on back on the floor, raise both knees to chest. Move legs in a circle, alternating sides. (*You are riding a bicycle*).

Step 2: Bring buttocks off the floor and raise legs in the air. Support buttocks with hands, elbows resting on floor. Do circular movements alternating legs as above. (*You are riding a bicycle in the air. You are a circus performer on a tightrope.*)

❀ E X E R C I S E 3

Step 1: Stand with feet together, toes slightly turned out, one arm resting on a barre or the back of a chair. Free arm raised to the side (second position). Point leg away from the barre to the front, toe pointed. Lift leg into the air, keeping knee straight. Then lower foot to the floor and close back to standing foot (first position). (*Point – lift – point – close.*) Turn around and do movement to other side.

Step 2: Standing as in Step 1, point toe to the front, make a circle on the floor with toe (rond de jambe). (*You are drawing a circle on the floor. Your big toe is like a piece of chalk. Make an even circle.*)

Imagery: Scissors, bicycle riding, chorus dancers, writing on the floor.

Relation to dance technique: Control of legs needed for all dance steps. Stretching legs, keeping knees straight, and pointing toes all require control, which needs to be practiced.

Head

❀ E X E R C I S E 1

Step 1: Sit on the floor, legs crossed in front. Turn head to the left, sharply turn head to the right. (*You are saying "No" very emphatically.*) Repeat.

Step 2: Move head slowly from right to left and back. Keep eyes fixed at one point in front.

Step 3: Move arms in various positions, let eyes and head follow arm movements. (*You are watching a butterfly and trying to catch it.*)

❀ E X E R C I S E 2

Step 1: Standing position, hands on shoulders, fix eyes on a spot in front. Shifting feet a little at a time, begin to turn body away from the front, keeping eyes on fixed spot. When spot is out of sight, whip head around to find spot again, bringing body around to the front. Recover with body facing front, eyes still fixed on the spot.

Repeat, turning the other way.

Imagery: Saying "No," watching a moving object, mechanical toy.

Relation to dance technique: The head must function as part of the dance movement. Fixing on a spot is the same as "spotting," which keeps dancers from getting dizzy when making turns.

All of the exercises in this chapter are offered as suggestions. Teachers may find other movements suitable for training the young dancer. Sequences may be varied and other images applied. What is important is for the teacher to be aware of the benefit of these exercises in preparing the young child for future work in dance.

Notes

1. Sandra Noll Hammond, *Ballet Basics*. 3rd ed. (Palo Alto, CA: Mayfield Publishing Co., 1993) p. 27.

3

LOCOMOTOR DELOPMENTAL MOVEMENT SEQUENCES

L ocomotor movements are those that take the body through space. They involve a transfer of weight from one foot to the other, or a lifting into the air and return to the same foot. There are generally considered to be eight locomotor movements that use the feet as a base.

All dance steps are combinations of these eight basic movements of locomotion: walk, run, leap, hop, jump, gallop, slide, and skip. There are, of course, ways of getting from one place to another that do not begin with the feet. Children will be quick to mention creeping, crawling, and rolling. A discussion of all of these, and how each can be developed into dance movements, follows. It is logical to start with movements that the child already knows. According to Ruth Murray, a pioneer in dance education:

> The new pattern should develop logically from the basic locomotor movement which has already been mastered. After this has been reviewed, the change of time intervals, accent, direction, or the addition of another movement can be gradually introduced, one at a time, as variations of the original movement.[1]

Under each category of locomotor movement the progression is from simple to complex. Some of the groups, three- and four-year-olds, for example, may not be able to coordinate well enough to do the more complicated sequences. The teacher must decide how far to go. By allowing the children to make up their own combinations of movement, the teacher can see the level at which they are operating, and can be guided by that.

Walk—Run—Leap

The walk is the simplest and most natural form of locomotion. There is a transfer of weight from one foot to the other in an even rhythm. The tempo of children's walking varies, with younger children having a faster pace than older ones. The teacher should adjust the accompaniment (piano or drum) to the natural tempo of her group.

Walks

❀ **E X E R C I S E**

Starting position: Stand in a circle facing the line of direction. (*Put your right arm into the circle, now face away from that arm, so you are ready to move around the circle, all facing the same way. Put your arm down.*) Young children may need help getting into position.

Step 1: Walk in a circle, following the beat of a drum. Change tempo as the drum changes. (*When the drum goes fast, you go fast. When the drum goes slow, you go slow. Take—one—step—every—time—you hear the drum.*) Arms swing naturally in opposition to legs.

Step 2: Walk on tiptoes. A lighter rhythm instrument, such as a triangle, can be used to accompany tiptoe walks.

Step 3: Walk four times and tiptoe four times. Alternate drum and triangle, playing four times each.

Step 4: Take low steps, bending knees and lowering body while walking. Alternate with high, tiptoe steps.

Step 5: Take fast, tiptoe steps. (*Little-teeny-tiptoe-steps.*)

Step 6: Try all of the above going backwards.

Step 7: Ballet walk. Walk with stretched toes, putting toes on the floor first instead of heels. Back and head must be well lifted. Combine with arm movements (see Exercise 2 of Arms, p. 26).

Relation to dance technique: Keeping time, both rhythm and tempo, with the accompaniment is essential in all types of dance. Counting the number of steps (whole, tiptoe) is getting ready for learning choreographed dances. The various qualities of walks are used in different kinds of dances. The ballet walk is part of all ballet dancing.

See also Appendix: Exercises, Activities, and Themes That Can Be Used to Enhance Learning in Academic Areas, Number Concepts, p. 98.

Runs and Leaps

A run carries the body through space by transferring its weight from the ball and toes of one foot to the ball and toes of the other. The body is lifted completely off the floor for a brief time during this transfer. The toes point forward and the body is inclined slightly forward. The arms, slightly bent at the

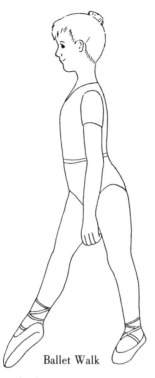

Ballet Walk

elbow, swing in opposition to the leg movement.

A leap is a run in which the upward and forward direction is increased as much as possible, with greater suspension in the air. The front leg extends forward, the knee leading, and the foot reaches forward to land. The rear leg extends backward and, upon landing, swings vigorously ahead into the next lift.

✿ E X E R C I S E

Starting position: As in Exercise of Walks, the circle should be reversed, that is, go in the opposite direction from time to time. (*Turn and go the other way.*)

Step 1: Take light, running steps in a circle, arms raised to the side. (*Push the floor with your toes.*)

Step 2: Continue running and count *1-2-3, 1-2-3, 1-2-3* (*drum accents the first beat*). Make the step on *1* heavier. This becomes a waltz. Remaining in the circle, lean into the circle as the heavy step is taken on the inside foot; lean away from the circle as the heavy step is taken on the outside foot. If group can do this at a faster tempo, waltz music may be played (e.g., "Skaters Waltz," "Waltz of the Flowers" from Tchaikovsky's *Nutcracker*).

Step 3: Make running steps bigger and push off the ground and ahead. This is a leap.

Step 4: Try leaping over a stick, rope, or beanbag. Coming across the room, children take turns one at a time. Run to the object and then leap, making one leg extend forward while the other extends backward going over the object on the floor. A cymbal can accompany the leap. Each child gets a chance to play the cymbal for the next child in line to run and leap. To gain proper distance and height for a leap, the momentum offered by preliminary running steps is necessary.

Leaping

Imagery: Animal movements, especially deer or tigers, horses leaping over fences, racers, gymnasts.

Relation to dance technique: Running steps are part of many ballets. Accented runs become waltzes. Running is a part of the Schottische and other folk dances. Leaps are often the most exciting part of a ballet. To achieve elevation, the leap (grand jeté) must be practiced along with pliés, foot exercises, and so forth.

See also Appendix: Exercises, Activities, and Themes That Can Be Used to Enhance Learning in Academic Areas, Number Concepts; Exploring Science, pp. 98; 101.

Hop—Jump

A hop carries the body upward into space by lifting it into the air from a takeoff on one foot and returning to the same foot. Ankles and toes are important in helping to push off from the floor. Like runs and leaps, knee bends (pliés, see Exercise 4 of Stretch—Bend, p. 21) should precede hops and jumps as warm-ups.

Jumps take off from both feet and land back on both feet. On landing, the weight is transferred quickly from the toes to the balls of the feet and then to the heels. This sequence is reversed on the takeoff.

Hopping

Hops

EXERCISE

Step 1: Lift up one leg and push off the floor using toes and ankles of the other foot. After landing on same foot, repeat as many times as possible. Try the same action on the other foot. (*How many times can you hop on your left foot? How many times can you hop on your right foot?*)

Step 2: While hopping on one foot, see what can be done with the free leg. The free leg can be bent up high in front or to the side; it can be extended forward, sideward, or backward; it can be bent at the knee and brought in so that the toe is touching the hopping leg.

Step 3: Using children's improvisations in Step 2, an Irish jig can be created (use for music "The Irish Washerwoman" or a similar jig). Hop on one foot and make different combinations with the other foot and leg, such as: (1) Touch free foot to the floor in front, then bend knee and bring foot to touch calf of hopping leg. Do same to the side. Repeat; (2) Touch free foot to floor in front, then to the side and repeat; (3) Touch free foot to the front, then bend knee and raise free leg high in front. Repeat.

Imagery: Irish dancers, hopscotch, birds hopping.

Relation to dance technique: As will be seen in the following sections, hops are an integral part of many dance steps. It is not often that hopping, per se, appears for any long period of time in a dance. The skill of hopping, however, involves balance and coordination. Young children (three-year-olds) may not be able to hop without holding on to something or someone. They should practice in this way because when children can hop well on each foot, they will be ready to skip.

See also Appendix: Exercises, Activities, and Themes That Can Be Used to Enhance Learning in Academic Areas, Social Learning, p. 100.

Jumps

❀ E X E R C I S E

Step 1: Beginning with pliés, bounce knees and straighten. (*Bend-and-straight bend-and-straight and-bounce-and-bounce.*) Tempo increases. Body should be erect, knees going over toes, toes only slightly turned out.

Step 2: When knees straighten, rise to toes, bend and stretch knees, making sure that back does not lean forward on the bend.

Step 3: Push off the floor into small jumps.

Step 4: Take two small jumps and one big one, landing on both feet each time. (*Bounce-and-bounce-and-jump.*) Use drum to accent the last beat.

Step 5: Start in crouched position, both feet on floor, knees bent as far as possible. Singing or playing "Pop Goes the Weasel," have children jump up on the word "Pop."

Imagery: Jack-in-the-Box (Step 5), jumping rope, rabbits, kangaroos, birds, high-jumping gymnasts.

Relation to dance technique: As with hopping, jumps are used in combination with other locomotor movements, rather than doing multiple jumps together. But the technique of executing a good jump improves coordination and balance. Elevation is a desirable ability in dance. Boys seem to achieve it better than girls, and they enjoy this vigorous activity.

See also Appendix: Exercises, Activities, and Themes That Can Be Used to Enhance Learning in Academic Areas, Number Concepts; p. 98.

Gallop — Slide — Skip

Gallops, slides and skips are frequently considered to be combinations of the more basic steps of walking, running, hopping, or jumping. Although they can be broken down into these elements, I consider them to be part of the basic locomotor movements.

One reason for saying this is that they appear frequently in children's games and free-play activities, without any formal instruction. They are also forerunners of ballet and folk dance steps. Therefore, they may be considered "ancestor movements."

The term "ancestor movements" was first used by two fine ballet teachers, Beatrice Sutter and Anne Rechter:

> If we remove the style and design characteristics and reduce the Ballet movements to their basic components, we find that Ballet is really a stylized development of natural movements or folk movements. These early movements and steps are the "ancestors" of those we know today."[2]

I have applied this concept to the presentation of dance technique throughout this book, since I feel that it provides a valid approach to teaching young children. Table 3 (pp. 36, 37) presents specific ancestor locomotor movements, defines them, and gives their ballet descendants.

Gallops

❀ E X E R C I S E

A gallop is a combination of a walk and a run. However, it should not be taught this way because very young children may gallop even before they walk. A happy toddler jogs along in a galloping motion, and three- and four-year-olds gallop in place of a skip whenever they hear an uneven rhythm.

Step 1: While they are seated on the floor, have the children clap a galloping rhythm:

Step 2: Allow the children to gallop any place in the room. This is lots of fun, but they must learn not to bump into one another.

Step 3: A gallop can be extended into a step-leap by extending the running step and slowing the tempo. Try this by having the children come across the floor one at a time. The leap will always come on the same foot, so the children should begin stepping on the opposite foot the second time they try this.

Imagery: Obviously, galloping suggests horses. *What kind of horse do you want to be?* (racehorses, circus horses, policemen's horses, etc.; see the story of "The Little Rocking Horse," p. 85.) *What other kinds of animals may gallop?*

Relation to dance technique: Many folk dances use a gallop or slide, which is related to gallop but done sideways (see p.38). The extension of the gallop into a step-leap is an excellent way to introduce, or to improve, leaping.

TABLE 3

Ancestor Locomotor Movements

Forward

Ancestor Movements	Definiton	Ballet Descendant
1. Natural Walk	One foot remains on the ground, while the other foot moves forward, then shift weight	Pas marché, or Stylized Balletic Walk (springy, with pointed toes)
Other Forms		
Lunge	A walking step, falling forward onto a bent knee	Pas Tombé
Walking Tiptoe (Tiptoe Walk)	Short steps on half toe	Walking on demi-pointes, preparation for chainé turns
2. Running	Springing from one foot to the other. Both legs in air for short time, body tilted forward	Balletic run, jeté fondu (with"4" design of leg)
Other Forms		
Prancing	Exaggerated run, high lift of knees	Pas Emboité (with front attitude design and pointed toes)
Leaping	Large, high, running step	All balletic leaps such as grand jeté
3. Hopping	Springing from one foot, coming down on the same foot	All Balletic hops, temps levé, arabesques temps levé, ballonnés
Other Forms		
Step-hop, skip		
4. Step-Close	Step-Close feet together	Glissade
Leap-Close	Spring from 2 feet to 1 foot	Sissonne ouverte, Sissonne fermé(close feet after landing)
Other Forms		
Sliding	Rapid step, close, first foot brushes floor before weight goes on it	Chassé
Two-Step	Step-together, step	Balletic Polka (hop and two-step)
5. Jumping	Spring from both feet to both feet (usually a closed foot position)	Sauté (all positions), Soubresaut

(continued on next page)

TABLE 3

Ancestor Locomotor Movements
(continued)

Sideward

Ancestor Movements	Definition	Ballet Descendant
Leaping	Leaping sideways or diagonally	Pas Jeté
Step-Close	Stepping sidward, then place feet together	With brushing movement, forms glissade
Sliding	Rapid side-close; first foot brushing floor before weight goes on it	Chassé
High Gallop	High, springy, step-close	Pas de Chat
Leap-Close	Springing from both feet to one foot	Sissonne ouverte, Sissonne fermé (close feet after landing)
Jump	Jump from two feet to two feet	Soubresaut

Spring

Combining Body Design and Locomotor Movements

Try combining locomotor or travelling movements; first with arm designs, then with torso and head designs. For example, rocking movements with opening and closing arm movements, galloping and a high horseshoe or 3rd position arm design. Other effective designs are bending designs and walking, stretching designs and running.

From Beatrice Sutter and Anne Rechter, *Ballet for Chidren* (Waldwick, NJ: Hoctor Dance Records, 1966), pp. 12 – 13.

Slides

✿ E X E R C I S E

A slide is a sideways gallop.

Starting position: Two children face each other and take hands.

Step 1: Starting with the foot that is toward the direction in which they will be going, go across the floor with a step-slide-step, getting off the floor on the running part of the step. The uneven rhythm of the gallop is used here as well.

Step 2: Slide back across the room beginning with the opposite foot.

Step 3: Slide across the floor four times, then stamp three times. Slide back, beginning with the opposite foot, four times and stamp three times.

Imagery: Square or folk dancing, sliding on the ice.

Relation to dance technique: A slide is already a dance step. Used in conjunction with simple stamping, it becomes a pattern that children must learn to count. Relating to a partner is an important dance experience.

See also Appendix: Exercises, Activities, and Themes That Can Be Used to Enhance Learning in Academic Areas, Number Concepts, p. 99.

Skips

✿ E X E R C I S E

A skip is a combination of a hop and a walk, done in an uneven rhythm similar to the gallop rhythm. Beginning with a walking step, the hop on the same foot takes the body into the air and returns it on the same foot. The other foot then steps forward into the next walking step followed by the hop.

Although this analysis is correct, there are better ways to teach a skip to young children. Three-year-olds will not be able to master this step, since they do not have the coordination to hop and return on one foot. They will gallop to the uneven rhythm until they can hop with ease on both feet. Some children can skip with one foot but not the other. They will do a one-sided skip-step-skip-step. If asked to hop on one foot, they will be able to do it on the foot on which they were able to skip, but not on the other foot. These children should be asked to hop on the weak foot, holding on to something, if necessary.

Step 1: Walking in a circle (see Walks, p. 30) in time with the drum. An even beat is played.

Step 2: Take each walking step with a little bounce. (*A bouncy-bouncy-bouncy-walk.*) Drum now plays a double beat.

Step 3: Bounce higher and lift off the floor. Drum now changes to an uneven beat (see Gallops, p. 35). Children are now skipping.

Step 4: Walk four times and then skip four times. Drum plays an even beat four times and an uneven skip rhythm four times.

Skipping

Step 5: Skip with knees brought up high in front. Then skip with free leg extended to the back. Skip and turn in a circle. (*Make up your own kind of skip.*)
Imagery: Children playing. Many songs about skipping can be used, for example, ("Skip to the Barber Shop to Buy a Penny Candy," "Skip to My Lou," "Looby-Loo."
Relation to dance technique: Stylized skipping is frequently used in combination with other locomotor movements (see Combining Locomotor Movements, p. 41.).
See also Appendix: Exercises, Activities, and Themes That Can Be Used to Enhance Learning in Academic Areas, Number Concepts, p. 99.

Crawl—Creep—Roll

The crawl, creep, and roll are locomotor movements that do not begin with the feet, but, nevertheless, do take the body from one place to another in space.

All of these activities precede other locomotor movements in the development of young children, but they are discussed last because they are not usually considered basic to dance steps, as are other locomotor movements. They do, however, appear in some dances. Young children feel comfortable doing them, even though they may be hesitant to participate in other movement explorations. Getting down flat on the floor seems to impart a sense of security to children, which may take them back to the warmth and comfort of infancy.

Crawling

❀ E X E R C I S E

This is the first locomotor activity performed by infants. Lying flat on the stomach, the arms and legs are used to propel the body forward.

Imagery: Worms, snakes, alligators, seals, crawling through tunnels, soldiers in battle and so forth.

Relation to dance technique: Frequently, the use of floor-level movement is used for dramatic effects of various kinds.

See also Appendix: Exercises, Activities, and Themes That Can Be Used to Enhance Learning in Academic Areas, Exploring Science, pp. 101-102.

Creeping

❀ E X E R C I S E

In creeping, children raise the abdomen from the floor and support themselves on their hands and knees. In this position, they propel themselves forward, using alternate arms with opposing leg movements (cross pattern).

This exercise is used in some of the perceptual-motor training for children with physical handicaps or learning disabilities. The alternating use of arms with legs is an essential coordination, relating to body awareness and sense of laterality.

Imagery: Cats, other four-legged animals, babies, turtles, spiders.

See also Appendix: Exercises, Activities, and Themes That Can Be Used to Enhance Learning in Academic Areas, Exploring Science, pp. 101-102.

Rolling

❀ E X E R C I S E

A roll is a locomotor movement in which the prone body is used as the basis for propulsion. The prone body is extended, the arms are stretched overhead, and the roll is made from front to back and continues from back to front. It may be done starting to the right or to the left and moving sideways.

A somersault or a cartwheel might also be considered in the category of a roll. A somersault begins with the placing of the back of the head on the floor and continuing a rolling movement forward. A cartwheel moves forward by throwing the body into the air and alternating hands and legs for contact with the floor. (*Left hand – right hand, right foot – left foot.*) The body turns around so that, on the contact of the last foot, it is facing front and ready to begin again. Raising the beginning foot before the first hand touches the ground gives momentum to the movement.

Imagery: Rolling logs, wheels, acrobats, clowns.

Relation to dance technique: Used occasionally for dramatic effect, the somersault or cartwheel represents vigorous activity and often changes the dynamics of a dance.

Combining Locomotor Movements

All dance steps are really combinations of the locomotor movements discussed above. Here are the common dance steps, and their origin in basic locomotor movement:

> Two-step: a walk done in the rhythm of slow–quick-quick, slow–quick-quick.
>
> Waltz: an even beat with accent on the first of three beats (3/4 time); can be a walk or a light, running step.
>
> Step-hop: a combination of a walk and a hop, usually performed in a forward direction; the rhythm is an even 2/4 time but one beat may be accented.
>
> Cha-cha: two slow and three quick walk steps; may be done forward, sideways, or backward, with variations such as crossing over standing foot on slow beats.
>
> Schottische: a combination of three running steps and a hop, usually in a forward direction.
>
> Polka: a combination of a hop and three springy walking steps, usually performed side-to-side.
>
> Mazurka: a combination of two springy walking steps and a hop; the accent is on the first walking step, with a secondary accent on the second walking step.

Although many of these combinations may be too difficult for the level at which the children are operating, it is good for the teacher to know what can be developed from the basic locomotor movements presented above. When the children are ready, suitable waltz, schottische, or mazurka music can be played and the teacher can demonstrate how the simple movements they are learning will lead to more complex dance steps. For those teachers who hope to lead their children into more complex ballet forms, Table 3 (p. 36) shows the ballet descendants that may be developed from "ancestor" locomotor movements. *See also* Appendix: Exercises, Activities, and Themes That Can Be Used to Enhance Learning in Academic Areas, Social Learning, p. 100.

Notes

1. Ruth L. Murray, *Dance in Elementary Education* (New York: Harper, 1953), p. 179.
2. Beatrice Sutter and Anne Rechter, *Ballet for Children* (Waldwick, NJ: Hoctor Dance Records, 1966), p. 9.

4

DEVELOPING RHYTHMIC AWARENESS

In chapters 2 and 3, exercises involving axial and locomotor movement were presented. Selections from each of these categories should be a part of every dance class. The following chapters contain a discussion of dance elements about which children need to be aware: rhythm, space, and movement quality. The second half of a dance class should be less structured where opportunity for improvisation with one or all of these elements is provided.

In the first chapter, How Movement Begins, the responses of infants to rhythmic sounds were discussed. Even before birth, the fetus responds to rhythm, and infants and toddlers are stimulated to move rhythmically whenever they hear music or even mechanical sounds with a strong beat. So the sense of rhythm is there at the beginning. Conscious awareness can be developed from these instinctive responses, so that rhythm becomes a part of children's dance, just as it is a basic component of all forms of adult dancing.

Although rhythm is easy to experience, it is hard to define. After having done some of the rhythmic activities described below, one child defined rhythm as "stopping and starting at different places and doing it the same way over again." This is very close to the adult concept of "repeated pattern of emphasis and pause" or "the regular recurrence of stress, accent, or beat" given in dictionaries.

Rhythm is made up of several component parts, such as tempo, dynamics, accent, pattern, and phrasing. This chapter defines each of these and gives activities that emphasize each one. However, there is much overlapping. As tempo changes, the dynamics of the rhythm is affected. Accent contributes heavily to pattern. The activities are an attempt to make children aware of these components, using terminology more suitable to the vocabulary with which they are familiar.

Tempo

Tempo is the rate of speed with which music or dance is performed. But tempo also manifests itself in life rhythms: in the heartbeat, in the respiratory system, and in all locomotor movements. Tempo is inherent as well in life situations, as when a man, walking toward a train station, sees the train approach and changes his pace to meet it. Change of tempo usually involves change in the emotional meaning of a musical composition or a dance.

The activities below are mainly focused on tempo, that is, changes from slow to fast or the reverse. But these changes also affect the feeling of the movement and the dynamics of the rhythm.

❀ A C T I V I T Y

Slow and Fast

Step 1: Walking in a circle, the children go slow or fast in time with the teacher's drum- or piano-playing. (*Take one step every time you hear a beat.*) The teacher should start with a tempo that suits young children, that is, it should be adjusted to the natural pace of the children's walking step. (*As the drum/piano goes fast, you go fast.*) Children accelerate movement until they are running. (*Now listen. The drum/piano is going slower—and walk, walk, walk. When the sound stops, you stop.*) Children slow up and stop moving when the drum or piano stops. This may take a little practice, since children find it hard to stop running once they have started. Holding a drumstick or hand up in the air gives a signal to cease all activity.

Step 2: Children hold on to one anothers' waists, making a "train." As the train leaves the station, it goes slowly. It picks up speed gradually until it is going fast. It slows down as it approaches the next station.

Step 3: Beginning in a crouching position, the children are "airplanes." With arms raised to the side, they slowly take off from the ground. They accelerate speed until they are "flying" around the room with arms outstretched. (*Now you are coming in for a landing.*) Accompaniment gets slower as children return to crouched position. Children may be numbered so that all do not "fly" at once. Teacher calls a number and that "airplane" takes off. Teacher again calls out numbers so that each child in turn returns to the floor.

Step 4: The image of a merry-go-round also demonstrates changes in tempo. Starting off slowly and accelerating in speed, the children run in a circle, simulating the up and down motion of the horses on a merry-go-round. Calliope music adds to the atmosphere but is not necessary. The music slows down as the merry-go-round comes to a stop.

All of these activities illustrate tempo. They need not be done consecutively; they might be used one at a time. Those dealing with trains or airplanes are suitable when a unit on "Transportation" is being discussed in the classroom. *See also* Appendix: Exercises, Activities, and Themes That Can Be Used to Enhance Learning in Academic Areas, Number Concepts; Social Learning, pp. 99; 100.

Dynamics

Dynamics refers to the varying degrees of energy used in a movement. Often the dynamic changes are reflected in loud and soft rhythmic sounds. The quality of movement changes as the dynamics changes, for example, increasing in energy to crescendo or diminishing to a quiet movement or pause. Increase in energy is often accompanied by increase in speed, but this need not always occur. Children often confuse fast and slow with loud and soft. The distinction between these two contrasting elements needs to be clarified through movement activities, thus leading to vocabulary enhancement.

The best example of a child's instinctive use of dynamics occurred in a beginning Head Start program in Mississippi. The children were taught the action game "It's a Mighty Pretty Motion" (see Activity 1 below), which has a strong, syncopated beat. Each child takes a turn doing a motion and the rest of the group follows it. One little girl volunteered, "I know a song that goes like that." She began to sing, "Give me more power, Lord." She repeated this phrase over and over, increasing in volume each time. Her body swayed and bounced as she sang and soon all of the children were doing the movements with her. She reached a crescendo, singing louder and moving vigorously. Then she decreased her movement and softened her singing. The whole class followed her lead. When she stopped, everyone stopped with her. This is an excellent example of a child's sense of dynamics, no doubt experienced by her in church services. The syncopated rhythm of "It's a Mighty Pretty Motion" reminded her of this. It was an exciting moment for the teacher and the class.

❀ A C T I V I T Y 1

"It's a Mighty Pretty Motion"
Starting position: Children stand in a circle facing the center. One child stands in the middle. As the song is sung, the child makes up a motion which everyone else follows.

> *It's a mighty pretty motion, de di do*
> *It's a mighty pretty motion, de di do*
> *It's a mighty pretty motion, de di do*
> *Rise, sugar, rise!*

Step 1: Song is repeated as children do motion initiated by the child in the middle. This is repeated a second time, as song is sung louder and faster. On the last "Rise, sugar, rise!," tempo is slowed and movement becomes quieter. Children raise arms forward and overhead on last line.

Step 2: Child in the middle then selects another child to go into the middle of the circle and start the motion.

❁ A C T I V I T Y 2

Thunderstorm

Step 1: Children do movements of play in the park. Some do swinging movements, some climbing, some go up and down in seesaw movements. Accompaniment on drum, piano, or record is a steady, even beat. A good record for this activity is "Golliwogg's Cakewalk" from Debussy's *Children's Corner Suite.*

Step 2: Beat accelerates as storm appears to be developing. Children cease playing activity and freeze in place while they listen.

Step 3: As storm arrives (music reaches a crescendo), children run for cover; teacher should designate corner of the room where "shelter" is.

See also Appendix: Exercises, Activities, and Themes That Can Be Used to Enhance Learning in Academic Areas, Exploring Science, p. 102.

❁ A C T I V I T Y 3

Responding to a Gong

The use of a large Chinese gong is a very good way to demonstrate dynamics. A piano or drum might be used, or several percussion instruments, increasing in number and volume as activity requires.

Step 1: Facing line of direction in a circle, children walk quietly around as gong is played softly.

Step 2: Gong increases in volume and tempo as children accelerate to a run.

Step 3: Gong is struck loudly and tone is allowed to ring until sound diminishes and stops. Children decrease speed of run and move toward center of circle, making steps slower and quieter. As sound stops, movement stops. Children should stand still, in a small circle, in close contact with each other.

Step 4: Another way to interpret the gong beat is to have each child move vigorously in his own way as the gong (or piano chord) is struck. As the sound dies away, the child's movement becomes smaller and quieter. When the gong sound stops, the child's movement stops and he "freezes" into a statue.

❁ A C T I V I T Y 4

Heavy and Tiptoe Steps

Step 1: Facing the line of direction in a circle, children walk in time to the drum or piano playing even quarter notes.

Step 2: Drum or piano slows to half notes. Children take slower, heavier steps.

Step 3: Speed increases to eighth notes with a softer sound (played with sticks, a triangle, or on the rim of the drum). Children walk fast on tiptoes.

Step 4: Children do eight heavy steps and sixteen tiptoe steps as accompaniment sets the pace. This can be interpreted as giant steps and tiptoe runs (as Jack runs away from the Giant). This entire activity can be incorporated in a dramatization of "Jack and the Beanstalk" (see Theme 1 of Classic Tales, p 82).

See also Appendix: Exercises, Activities, and Themes That Can Be Used to Enhance Learning in Academic Areas, Experiencing Music, p. 104.

❀ A C T I V I T Y 5

"The Three Bears"

Acting out the story "The Three Bears" demonstrates very well for young children the differences in dynamics of rhythm and movement. Father Bear walks with heavy, slow steps (half notes) and talks in a slow, deep voice. Mother Bear has a moderate pace (quarter notes) and moderate voice. Baby Bear takes little tiptoe steps (eighth notes) and talks in a quick, high voice.

The story "Three Billy Goats Gruff" can be used in the same way. As each goat crosses the bridge, he uses different size and weight steps.

Accent

Rhythmic accents might be described as additional force placed on one of the beats in a series. When counting beats in music or dance, there is a tendency for the first beat in a series of two, three, or four to be stronger than the others. These groups of beats are known as "measures," the first beat of each measure receiving added stress. These accents are called "regular."

Accents may also occur at other points in the measure. When the regular order is temporarily interrupted and accents are placed on normally unaccented or weaker parts of the measure, these accents are called "syncopated." Modern dance and jazz dance often employ syncopated accents. Children will respond to these differences in accent with appropriate movement. They do not have to be familiar with the terminology, but experience with various kinds of accents increases their awareness of rhythm and its contribution to dance.

❀ A C T I V I T Y 1

"Jack-in-the-Box"

As a first experience in the study of accent, young children enjoy playing "Jack-in-the-Box." They squat down, with feet remaining on the floor, as the teacher sings.

> *All around the cobbler's bench*
> *The monkey chased the weasel*

The weasel thought it was all in fun
"Pop" goes the weasel!

When the word "Pop" is heard, the children jump up and assume a funny position, like a clown. They "freeze" in that position as the teacher makes comments about their responses. The game is then repeated.

See also Appendix: Exercises, Activities, and Themes That Can Be Used to Enhance Learning in Academic Areas, Language Development, p. 96.

❀ A C T I V I T Y 2

Responding to a Cymbal

Step 1: Standing in one place, the class practices jumps by bouncing knees twice with feet on the floor and then jumping on the third beat. (*Bounce-and-bounce-and-jump!*) A child might be selected to play a cymbal on the third beat.
Step 2: Walking in a circle, the children combine one jump with three walks. The cymbal will be played on the first of each measure of four beats. (*Jump-walk-walk-walk.*) When doing children's names (see Activity 2 of Rhythmic Pattern below), the cymbal is used for the accented beat, such as *Steph-an-ie Jones.*
Step 3: Coming across the room from one corner to the other on the diagonal, children learn to leap by running and leaping over a stick or rope. As each one leaps, another child plays the cymbal when the leap occurs. The child leaping then takes the cymbal and plays it for the next child in line.

See also Appendix: Exercises, Activities, and Themes That Can Be Used to Enhance Learning in Academic Areas, Experiencing Music,   p. 104.

❀ A C T I V I T Y 3

Statues

Children run in a circle until they hear the accented beat. (*Run and run and run and hold.*) They then take a strong movement in their body and hold it as in a statue. As a variation, the children might wait for the accent as the teacher plays six eighth notes, and then the children take a strong movement on the accented beat. They hold this strong position until the accented beat is repeated in the next measure.

Rhythmic Pattern

Patterns exist whenever there is contrast between stressed and unstressed elements, and when this contrasting series is repeated. In music, the accent at the beginning of each measure creates a metrical pattern. In poetry and in speech there are rhythmic patterns that are usually repeated and can be identified by clapping the sounds. Pattern exists visually in art work and in designs. The activities that follow and those in the next chapter on space give children experience with all of these types of patterns.

According to Ruth Murray, "A rhythmic pattern in music or dance is a group of at least three beats with unequal time intervals, the beats following in uneven rather than even sequence. . . . The intervals must always have a mathematical relationship to each other and to an underlying pulse beat on which the pattern is built."[1] The best way to illustrate this concept with young children is by the use of rhythm instruments (see Activity 5, p. 52). When they are ready (at age five or six), the teacher might introduce the symbols of time, that is, notes. A walking time is represented by a quarter note, running by eighth notes. Thus, a pattern consisting of four walks and eight runs might be represented:

The runs must be exactly twice as fast as the walks, establishing a mathematical relationship. Thus, mathematical concepts can be strengthened through movement and rhythm.

✽ A C T I V I T Y 1

Walks and Runs

Step 1: The children follow the drum beat or piano while moving in a circle in a line of direction (as in Activity, Step 1 of Tempo, p. 44.)

Step 2: (*Now let's count the number of walking steps and the number of running steps.*) Teacher plays eight quarter notes and sixteen eighth notes, repeating the pattern over and over. (*We will count the running steps by saying "And" between two numbers, so we count:* 1 2 3 4 5 6 7 8 (walking)

and: 1 & 2 & 3 & 4 & 5 & 6 & 7 & 8 (running)
The runs are twice as fast as the walks, aren't they?
See also Appendix: Exercises, Activities, and Themes That Can Be Used to Enhance Learning in Academic Areas, Number Concepts, p.104.

With younger children (three- and four-year-olds), it is necessary for them only to feel the time being doubled. Older children might discover that sixteen is twice as much as eight.

✽ A C T I V I T Y 2

Names

Nothing is more meaningful to young children than their names. Three- and four-year-olds have just begun to know themselves as individuals, separate from the family unit. Five- and six-year-olds take great pride in their own identity and their own accomplishments. Children from deprived backgrounds often lack that sense of self and need to have it identified and reinforced before they are ready to learn.

For the teacher, an activity concerned with the children's names helps her to get to know the children in her class. She will need a big drum. One skin with a wooden frame (Wigman drum) is best, but a tom-tom or bongo-type drum is also suitable. A timpani beater with a felt top is desirable.

Starting position: Children sit cross-legged in a circle. Teacher sits in the middle of the circle with drum and beater held above floor level.

Step 1: (*The drum is going to say your name. Tell me your first and last name.*) The teacher goes around the circle, playing each child's name on the drum.

Step 2: (*Now I will play your name and then I will give you the beater and you will play it after me.*) Teacher holds the drum, but gives beater to each child in succession around the circle.

Can You Play Your Name on the Drum?

Step 3: Teacher picks names with interesting rhythms and asks the class to clap these names after hearing them on the drum. For example, Mel-an-ie John-son. (*How many beats [syllables] in Melanie's name?*) Then the children use individual instruments to play their names.

Step 4: (*Which beat is stronger? Can you clap that one louder?*) The strong beat is the accent.

Step 5: Children stand up and face in the line of direction. (*Put your left hand in the circle. Face away from it. Put the hand down. Can we walk to the rhythm of Melanie's name?*) It will take three fast steps and two slower ones. The class will then try walking to other names.

Step 6: It is possible to go from beating the rhythm of names to counting the beats (syllables). For example, Melanie Johnson's name has five beats. Three are fast and two are slower. (*How many beats altogether? Good! Then three and two make five.*) Thus, a rhythm session now becomes a lesson in arithmetic.

Step 7: (*How else might we make five? Yes, four and one make five. Can you do that in movement?*) The children make up combinations of walks, runs, hops, and jumps totaling five. (*Four walks and one jump make five. Four hops and one step make five. Show me another one.*)

See also Appendix: Exercises, Activities, and Themes That Can Be Used to Enhance Learning in Academic Areas, Number Concepts, p. 99.

Components of other numbers may be explored in this way. A mathematics lesson studying components of a number might end up with rhythmic exploration of that number. Younger children would start with "three," possibly using two walks and a jump. Older groups (five- and six-year-olds) might learn to write the combinations.

In one first-grade class, Heidi was asked to write the combinations on the blackboard as the rest of the class moved around the outside of the room making up new steps. She wrote:

$2 + 2 = 4$ for 2 walks, 2 jumps
$3 + 1 = 4$ for 3 walks, 1 jump
$4 + 0 = 4$ for 4 jumps, pause

"It's not fair!" said Heidi. "I'm working while everyone else is playing." Heidi considered writing to be hard work; making up numerical combinations in movement was "play." But learning mathematics can be fun when movement is involved.

❀ A C T I V I T Y 3

Developing a Waltz

Step 1: Facing line of direction in a circle children practice running in time to a beat (piano or drum plays even, moderately fast running rhythm).

Step 2: Children count by threes, clapping on the first beat (1-2-3, 1-2-3). They take a heavier running step on the count of one.

Step 3: Starting with the accented step on the foot toward the inside of the circle, children lean in that direction. The next accented run comes on the opposite foot, so the children lean toward the outside of the circle. It will take time for young children to accomplish this "triplet" rhythm owing to immature physiological development. The activity should be repeated frequently for short intervals.

Step 4: Step 3 can be slowed and a selection of waltz music can be played (e.g., "Waltz of the Flowers" from Tchaikovsky's *Nutcracker*). When the children can keep time with this, they are doing a waltz. Arm movements may be improvised, based on swinging in different directions, and children may move any place in the room, alone or with partners.

❀ A C T I V I T Y 4

Speech Patterns and Nursery Rhymes

As in Activity 2, where children created rhythms based on their names, other speech patterns can be used to create rhythms that children can move to, for example, "Beat my drum," "It's time to go to bed," "Doggie, doggie, get that bone."

Nursery rhymes make excellent patterns because of their familiarity and repetition. Some favorites to try stepping to are "Hot Cross Buns," "Sing a Song of Sixpence," "One, Two, Buckle My Shoe," "Mary Had a Little Lamb."

❀ A C T I V I T Y 5

Using Rhythm Instruments

In order to create a rhythm orchestra, instruments have to be introduced and the sounds they make explained. They should be distributed in a special order. Most kindergartens and nursery schools have sets of instruments, but not all of the instruments have a clear enough beat to be effective in a percussion orchestra.

There are four sets of preferred instruments.

Drums: Small hand drums with one skin and handles are desirable. Tom-toms and bongo (single, not two with different tones) drums may be used.

Tambourines: Very effective, since two sounds can be produced; one by shaking and one by hitting.

Sticks: Any type of wooden instrument that can be struck. An effective instrument can be made with two half-inch dowel sticks, about one foot long, which can be hit together.

Bells or Triangles: Tinkling sounds can be made by shaking bells or hitting triangles. Two spoons can be hit together to add to this section of the orchestra, if more instruments are needed.

The cymbal also belongs in this category, but only one or two should be allowed in the orchestra. They are used mainly for accents, and will drown out other instruments if used continuously.

After each instrument has been demonstrated, it is given out so that there are four sections of the orchestra. A good way to avoid confusion is to have the children sit in a semicircle with eyes closed; the teacher then places an instrument behind each child. When all are distributed, the children are told to pick up the instrument behind them. They may experiment with making the sound, but must be told to respond to a signal to stop playing and wait for directions. The teacher may say, *When I hold my beater up in the air, everyone* must stop playing and pay attention. It's as if I'm the conductor of the orchestra who holds up his baton to signal the orchestra members to wait to begin.

❀ A C T I V I T Y 6

"Frère Jacques (Brother John)"

Drums	"Are you sleeping, Are you sleeping,	Playing even, quarter notes
Tambourines	Brother John? Brother John?	Playing accented syllables: half notes
Sticks	Morning bells are ringing, Morning bells are ringing,	Playing twice as fast as drums: eighth notes
Bells	Ding, Dong, Ding Ding, Dong, Ding."	Playing on each beat: quarter notes
Cymbals		Playing only on first "Ding": accented first beat

The teacher leads this activity, letting each group have a chance to play alone. Later, they may play in succession, starting with the drums and adding each instrument group, one at a time, until all are playing together.

Four groups of dancers may be assigned to move with each part of the orchestra, moving only when their instrument is played. This is an excellent way to teach children the value of notes and to instill in them an awareness of the way an orchestra can keep in time and yet be playing different beats.

❀ A C T I V I T Y 7

Creating Rhythms

Step 1: The teacher sets the tempo, playing an even, steady beat on her drum.
Step 2: A child is selected to play her own rhythm, perhaps her name or a pattern from a nursery rhyme for example,

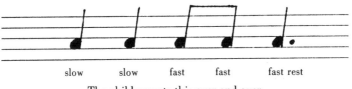

slow   slow   fast   fast   fast rest

The child repeats this over and over.

Step 3: The cymbal may play on the first beat of the pattern. Drums may play only the first two slow beats. Sticks and bells may play only the three fast beats. Tambourines may hit the skin on the slow beats and shake the jingles on the fast beats.
See also Appendix: Exercises, Activities, and Themes That Can Be Used to

Enhance Learning in Academic Areas, Number Concepts, p. 99.

Children may be assigned to dance to one of the instruments, as in Activity 6. Later, the child who makes up the rhythm may assign the parts for each group of instruments.

❀ A C T I V I T Y 8

Accompanying a Dancer

Starting position: Children with instruments sit in a semicircle, grouped together by instrument (as above).

Step 1: A dancer (perhaps, at the beginning, the teacher) stands in the middle of the semicircle. She tells the orchestra how she wants to be accompanied. (*e.g., Drums will play when I walk. Sticks will play when I run. Cymbals will play when I jump. Bells and tambourines will play when I spin around*).

Step 2: After a while, a child can be the dancer and can tell the orchestra how he wants to be accompanied. When the dancer stops moving, the orchestra must stop at the same time.

❀ A C T I V I T Y 9

Working in Pairs

Working with a Partner

Step 1: Children choose partners. One has a rhythm instrument and the other is the dancer.

Step 2: They practice by themselves, the child with the instrument accompanying the dancer. They may change places, letting the musician become the dancer.

Step 3: They come back to form a group and each pair takes a turn showing the rest of the group what they have created.

This activity can be done on a playground, if possible. In that way, the sounds will not interfere with one another as much, and other classes will not be disturbed.

Phrasing

A musical phrase, like a phrase in language, is an incomplete musical idea used in combination with another or several phrases to make a composition. A phrase is at least two measures long. Repeated or combined with other phrases, they create the form of composition, whether in music or dance.

The recognition of musical phrasing by children is another element of rhythmic learning. Dance movement should change as new musical phrases are introduced, or movements may repeat as phrases are repeated.

❀ A C T I V I T Y 1

Dramatizing Nursery Rhymes

The study of the musical phrase with young children might begin with the dramatization of simple songs or nursery rhymes. For example:

> *Little Miss Muffet sat on a tuffet,*
> *Eating her curds and whey,*
> *Along came a spider and sat down beside her,*
> *And frightened Miss Muffet away.*

Two children can act this out, one as Miss Muffet and the other as the spider.

It will be easy for the rest of the class to identify the phrases of the above rhyme, each line making up one phrase. The third phrase introduces the action of the spider. In the fourth phrase, Miss Muffet runs away. Children in the audience should clap at the beginning of each phrase.

Other appropriate nursery rhymes are suggested in Activity 4 of Rhythmic Pattern, p. 52.

See also Appendix: Exercises, Activities, and Themes That Can Be Used to Enhance Learning in Academic Areas, Language Development, p. 96.

❀ A C T I V I T Y 2

Moving with Partners

Step 1: Children choose partners and stand facing each other.

Step 2: Dancer 1 creates a movement that makes a rhythmic phrase. He does it one time and holds the final position (e.g., *Swing and swing, make an arm circle, and swing*).

Step 3: Dancer 2 repeats the movement of Dancer 1.

Step 4: Each dancer performs a movement alternately. Teacher's drum signals the time for partners to change.

Step 5: When phrasing is clearly established, the partners may make up different movements, rather than imitating the first dancer. Each child must remember to hold (i.e., "freeze") at the end of his movement phrase. This activity can assume the form of questions and answers in movement.

✸ A C T I V I T Y 3

Moving to Selected Music

Step 1: Class listens to a record or the piano playing a familiar musical selection or song. They clap at the beginning of each new phrase. Ballads and folk songs often introduce a second part after the first part has been repeated. There is a return to the first part after the middle part (AABA). Children should be able to identify each theme as it is introduced.

Step 2: The class is divided in half. Each group will move on one theme in the music. A good selection for this is Fritz Kreisler's *Caprice Viennois*. There is a clearly defined swinging theme and an alternating theme that strongly suggests running steps. Each group is assigned one of these themes. They are to take turns moving when they hear their theme (swinging or running) and remain still while the other group moves.

All these activities relating to tempo, dynamics, accent, rhythmic pattern, and phrasing are aimed at making children more aware of the contributions of rhythm to dance and music. The focus has been on the components of rhythm, but remember that there is much overlap and it is difficult to separate them.

Children need not become familiar with the terminology, but the activities will heighten rhythmic awareness. By identifying the components, the teacher can see how these simple activities relate to the overall structure of music and dance.

Notes

1. Ruth L. Murray, *Dance in Elementary Education* (New York: Harper, 1953), p. 234.

I want to acknowledge the contributions, throughout this chapter, of Emile Jaques-Dalcroze's Eurhythmics to my understanding of the relationship between music and dance. Having studied with a Delcroze teacher, I have assimilated and used some of his innovative methods for teaching music through movement to children.

5

EXPLORING SPACE

M ovement is the essential ingredient of space perception. It is by moving that infants learn to differentiate themselves from the outside world (see Developing Sensorimotor Skills, p. 3). In the early years, "the young child is at the center of his spatial universe and perceives space in relation to himself. Hence he builds relationships based upon self: self in relation to the dimensions inside a car, to parts of a doorway, or to a table or chair. By observing his own body and the relationship among objects in space to parts of his body, he relates himself to the space outside himself."[1]

From the very beginning of a dance or movement class, children need to be made aware that they define space by their very presence. The teacher might say, *Find your own space on the floor. Be sure you are not touching anyone.* After some activities moving in their own space, the children may become aware of others moving around them. They learn to relate to a partner, to create designs in space, and to construct group configurations.

The activities described in this chapter deal with elements of spatial awareness. Beginning with body shapes, the pattern or design that a movement makes in space will be explored. These patterns are also created by direction of the body, levels, relationships to partners or groups, and floor patterns.

Shape

The shape of the body communicates a great deal emotionally and aesthetically. Figures in sculpture present a mood, as does, for example, Rodin's *The*

Thinker. If children can visit a museum to see sculpture, or be shown pictures in class, they will begin to understand something about body shape—the beauty of the human body and its expressive quality.

Dancers convey some of these same attributes. The line of a ballet dancer's body in movement or in a set pose is one of the elements that gives form and beauty to the dance. In duets or in group compositions, the relationship among the dancers creates a pattern that can be compared with a painting or sculpture. Line and design experienced through movement can carry over into appreciation of other art forms.

❀ A C T I V I T Y 1

Moving in a Prescribed Space

Step 1—Children need to be aware of their own bodies as taking up space. They can explore the space around them by moving in an imaginary box. The teacher's drum or a chord on the piano can signal the children to change positions. They must stay within the confines of the imaginary box. The teacher may encourage exploration. (*Can you reach the corner up above you? Can you now reach the floor behind you?*) Children may stand, kneel, or lie down, but the perimeters of the box need to be defined ahead of time. (*We should be able to tell if your box is tall or wide, big or little, by the way you show us the space you are moving in.*)

Step 2—Hoops may be used to define a space. Each child stands inside a hoop that has been laid on the floor. He makes small movements inside the hoop. At a command, he steps outside the hoop but with one foot still inside. Movements now are large and free. The children should sense the difference between moving in a confined space and moving outside of it.

❀ A C T I V I T Y 2

Forming Shapes

Step 1—The children make circles with their bodies or parts of them. (*See how many circles can be made. John is making a circle with his pointer finger. Suzie is making a large circle in the air with both arms. Sharon is making a circle on the floor with her toes. If she had a piece of chalk between her toes, could we see the circle?*)

Step 2—(*Triangles are sharp and angular. How many ways can you make triangles with your body?*) Children explore making triangles with hands clasped in front of them, with elbows pointed, with hands on hips, or with legs spread forming a triangle with the floor, and so forth.

Step 3—Squares or rectangles are more difficult to make in space. It may require two children working together to form these shapes.

See also Appendix: Exercises, Activities, and Themes That Can Be Used to Enhance Learning in Academic Areas, Number Concepts, p. 99.

❀ A C T I V I T Y 3

Statues

This is a game often played by children on the playground. It can be used to develop an awareness of body shape if the teacher focuses on the design formed by the "statues."

One individual (perhaps the teacher) stands in the middle of a large space. She takes one hand of a child and spins him around by pivoting her own body quickly. When she lets go of his hand, the child falls into a position and "freezes," as in a statue. Each child has a chance to be spun around. The teacher calls attention to interesting shapes formed by the "statues."
See also Appendix: Exercises, Activities, and Themes That Can Be Used to Enhance Learning in Academic Areas, Art Experiences. p. 103.

❀ A C T I V I T Y 4

Using Props

Each child holds a dowel stick, about three feet long, firmly at both ends. He explores the shapes his body can make using the dowel. A signal on the drum or chord on the piano can indicate time to change and create a new design.

Design with a Stick

Ropes or elastic cords can be used in place of dowels, which may be dangerous for younger children to handle.

Direction

The direction of movement of the body has a strong impact on movement quality. Straight forward movements imply force and strength. Backward movements may denote fear. Sideward movements can be pleasant and relaxed.

Children should have experience moving in all directions, and should become aware of the impact of direction on their movement.

Children like to explore different directions in movement in their daily lives. Five-year-olds on their way to school may weave "scallop"-fashion from one side of the sidewalk to the other, touching the hood of each car parked along the curb. This shows an awareness of the possibilities of space. Children should be allowed time to explore space and direction on their own.

✾ A C T I V I T Y 1

Getting from Here to There

Starting position—Children line up along the wall facing the center of the room.

Step 1—(*How can you get from where you are to the other side of the room?*) Children take turns, one at a time, moving across the room. (*You need not go in a straight line. Try another way.*) Children are also encouraged to move sideways, backward, on knees, and so forth.

Step 3—(*How did that way of moving make you feel?*) Children discuss how it felt, and how that way of moving might be used in a dance.

✾ A C T I V I T Y 2

Being Pulled by a String

Step 1—(*Feel that a string is attached to some part of your body and let that part pull you through space.*) The use of strongly rhythmic music (rock, or African drums) can make this a lively exercise.

Step 2—Individual children are selected to demonstrate how a part of their body led them. Ear or elbow leading might create sideward movements. Walking forward with chin leading may create a "stuck-up" look. Going backward with buttocks leading could be comic or fearful.

Step 3—(*How did that way of moving make you feel? Would it be a good idea to create movements like that if you were making a dance?*) Children discuss these questions.

✾ A C T I V I T Y 3

Locomotor Movements in Different Directions

Step 1—Beginning in a circle facing the line of direction, children perform locomotor activities (as in Exercise for Walks, p. 30 and Exercise for Runs-Leaps, p. 31. After a while, teacher will signal to do the same movement going backward. (*Let's walk backward, taking the same size steps that you were doing forward. Don't look back. Keep eyes forward and watch a spot on the wall. Try to keep in the circle. And now let's go forward again.*)

Repeat activity with runs and leaps. Younger children (three- and four-year-olds) may have difficulty with leaps going backward, but they may have fun

P.S. NEW DESIGNS

JCHUES -
— C- SHUES

— WHATSAPP -
— PACC - SEND TO OTHER ...

3 WAYS!
TO JUMP
ROLL
CEPH

M5 TOGETHER   FAST - SLOW —
                                    SPIN -

WIND UP TOYS

I LIKE .. CAN YOU ALSO DO..
STOU MC, CAN YOU, LETS
HOW MANY WAYS CAN YOU...
SWING

SENSITIVE / PARENTS
— MAKING EMOTIONAL in DRAWING BELONG
LOVE / SAD — DANCE ...

trying. (*See if you can do this. Backward is harder than forward, isn't it?*)

Step 2—Coming across the floor on the diagonal, one at a time, children skip forward for four skips and then skip in a small circle for four skips. (*You should be facing forward again after the four skips in a circle. And-skip-two-three-four, and-turn-two-three-four.*)

Step 3—With partners holding hands, children slide across the room, two at a time. They begin with the foot facing the line of direction and move sideways. Coming back, they start with the opposite foot. Galloping or skipping music can be used.

See also Appendix: Exercises, Activities, and Themes That Can Be Used to Enhance Learning in Academic Areas, Number Concepts, p. 99.

❀ A C T I V I T Y 4

Making a Square

Step 1: Children go in different directions, facing forward all the time (body plane remains frontal). (*Find your own space. Now take two steps forward, turn and take two steps to the side, turn and take two steps backward, turn and take two steps to the other side, turn to the front again and take two steps forward.*)

Step 2: Children change directions, facing front all the time without turning. (*Now we are going to make a square, facing front all the time. Take three steps forward, now take two sliding steps to the side—moving sideward, step together, step together. Now take three steps backward, now two sliding steps to the other side.*)

Step 3: Children do an oppositional stretch. (*Let's add arm movements and body stretches to the square. As you go forward, reach your arms backward and lean your head back. When you go sideward, reach your arms to the opposite side, with one arm over your head. When you go backward, stretch forward and reach your arms in front of you.*) They may not be ready to execute this accurately, but they will begin to know directions and the natural body positions that evolve from them.

See also Appendix: Exercises, Activities, and Themes That Can Be Used to Enhance Learning in Academic Areas, Number Concepts, p. 99.

❀ A C T I V I T Y 5

Focus

Focusing the eyes on a set point helps the individual to achieve direction. When eyes are unfocused, when children look at the ground or around the room as they move, they are likely to become dizzy or disoriented. Even for experienced dancers, a movement will have less effect if they do not focus their eyes to sustain the directional impact of the movement. For these reasons, activities to develop focus are included in this section on directions.

Step 1: Each child finds a corner of the room to move to. He must focus his eyes and move slowly toward it. Several children may move at one time. They must follow their own direction but be aware of the others around them.

Step 2: Each child is then to find another corner, focus upon it, and find another way to get there. They are to continue until all four corners of the room have been reached.

Step 3: Skipping across the room on a diagonal, one child at a time, children change head position after a certain number of skips. They may begin with eyes forward, but change to looking over the shoulder while still skipping forward. Every time there is a loud beat on the drum, they change focus but keep skipping in the same direction. (*What happens to your sense of direction if you look another way as you move?*)

Step 4: (*Can you keep your eyes on one spot on the wall and still turn around in a circle? This is called "spotting" and all dancers have to learn to do it so that they can keep turning without getting dizzy.*) This is difficult and takes a great deal of practice, but young children may be introduced to the concept. They can try to practice it at home whenever they like. They will find out for themselves when the head should snap around quickly to keep the spot on the wall in focus as they turn.

Level

In addition to changes in direction (forward, backward, sideways), changes in movement can be made on different levels in space. Children can explore moving on high, medium, and low levels. Too often, dances are done in an upright, standing position, but dance compositions are more interesting if more than one level is used. Opportunities for moving on knees, at floor level, or high on tiptoes should be included in class activities.

❀ A C T I V I T Y 1

Exploring Levels

Step 1: Axial movements done during exercises in Chapter 1 should be experienced on different levels. (*What kinds of stretches can you do while lying on the floor?*) Some children may demonstrate a floor stretch while others repeat it after them.

Step 2: Standing, children stretch in various directions, keeping body at the middle (standing) level. Another medium level is achieved beginning on knees. One or two children may be selected to demonstrate.

Step 3: A high level can be attained through overhead stretching and by jumping in various ways.

Step 4: Using the imagery of painting a wall, children use an imaginary brush to reach high, sideways, and low on the wall. (*Take long, even strokes. Feel the weight of the brush as it moves in space. Now paint the ceiling. Stretch to reach it. What parts of your body are you using in addition to your arms?*)

✿ A C T I V I T Y 2

Concentric Circles

Step 1: Children form three concentric circles. The outside circle stand, the middle circle kneels, the inside circle sits on their feet.

Step 2: At a signal (drum beat or chord on the piano) from the teacher, the groups change—outside circle kneels, middle circle sits on their feet, inside circle stands up.

Step 3: Outside circle sits on their feet, middle circle stands up, and inside circle kneels.

At each step, the teacher should call attention to the designs made by the three groups. Arm movements may be added, one for each level (e.g., overhead for standing, to sides for kneeling, down on floor for sitting) when children are ready.

✿ A C T I V I T Y 3

Responding to Sounds

Step 1: The teacher will play high, medium, and low sounds on the piano; xylophone may be used or a combination of drum (low), sticks, or maracas (medium), and bells or triangles (high). Children identify low, medium, and high sounds even when they are played in different orders.

Step 2: (*Move on the same levels as you hear the sounds. When I play a different sound, you will move again and change levels.*)

Step 3: Teacher changes tempo so that children move to different levels in a steady flow. (*Listen to changes and use your whole body in space.*)

✿ A C T I V I T Y 4

Two Children in Opposition

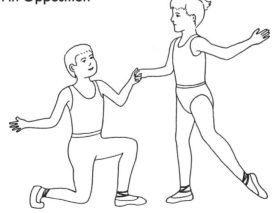

Two Children in Opposition

Starting position: Two children stand opposite each other.

Step 1: First child assumes a position at high, medium, or low level.

Step 2: Second child assumes a position that is on a different level.

Step 3: At a signal from the teacher (drum beat or piano chord), they change positions and levels. (*Watch each other to see that you are on different levels. See what designs your positions make in space.*)

See also Appendix: Exercises, Activities, and Themes That Can Be Used to Enhance Learning in Academic Areas, Art Experiences, p. 103.

✽ A C T I V I T Y 5

Relating to Others Using Different Levels

Step 1: The class is divided into groups of four. All move together following the beat of the drum. When the drum stops, children "freeze" at various levels.

Step 2: Children are numbered one through four. Number one assumes a position at one of the levels.

Step 3: Each child in succession assumes a position relating to each other but at different levels. (*As you move through space, stop at a level that is different from the others in your group.*)

Step 4: Children hold positions until all four have done their movements. Teacher calls attention to the interesting designs formed when moving at different levels.

Using Different Levels

Relating to Others

When children become aware of spatial relationships, they are ready to work as partners and in groups. We have already seen in the previous two activities that working in different levels requires children to relate to each other. Other group activities follow, in which spatial relationships are stressed while working with others.

❀ A C T I V I T Y 1

Mirroring

Two children stand facing each other. As one moves the other becomes a "mirror," doing the same movements at the same time. If each child concentrates on the other, it will be difficult to tell who has initiated the movement. A recording of slow, smooth music should be used. This is an activity used for various age levels, including adults, in both dance and drama classes. It develops concentration and awareness of others.
See also Appendix: Exercises, Activities, and Themes That Can Be Used to Enhance Learning in Academic Areas, Social Learning, p. 100.

❀ A C T I V I T Y 2

Opposition Movements

Step 1: Two children stand facing each other as in Activity 1. As child 1 moves, child 2 reacts to the movement. For example, if child 1 does a pushing movement, child 2 moves backward as if being pushed. Both members of the pair are to remain in one place on the floor.
Step 2: Various axial movements may be tried. Child 2 should initiate movement after a while, with child 1 reacting.
Step 3: (*Be aware of the shapes you are making in space. Use different levels.*) After a while, pairs will show the rest of the class what they have done. Class will make comments about design and the way the pair related to each other.

❀ A C T I V I T Y 3

Machines

Step 1: (*Have you ever seen machines in a factory? As one gear goes around, another part of the machine may go up and down in the same rhythm. Now we will make a machine. Each of you will do a different movement but you will be able to relate to each other.*)
Step 2: One child stands in the middle of the room and starts a movement.
Step 3: A second child joins in, moving close to child 1, but not touching.
Step 4: Several more children join in, one at a time. The "machine" might be

made up of six or seven children, all moving in different ways but all relating to each other and to the beat of the drum.

❋ A C T I V I T Y 4

Making a Picture

Step 1: The class is divided into groups of three or four. Each group takes a few minutes to plan their "picture." It might be an abstract design in space, or it might have story content, for example, a teacher and some pupils in a class, a game of tennis, or workers constructing a building.

Step 2: Child 1 assumes a position on the first beat of the drum or piano chord. Child 2 improvises a complementary movement on the second beat, followed by the third and/or fourth child. They hold the "picture."

Step 3: The rest of the class evaluates the picture. If it has story content, they might guess what the "picture" is about. The relationship among members of the performing group needs to be stressed as well as the overall design.

See also Appendix: Exercises, Activities, and Themes That Can Be Used to Enhance Learning in Academic Areas, Art Experiences. p. 103.

Floor Pattern

Whenever individuals or groups move through space, they create designs on the floor. A complex dance composition relies heavily on the plan the choreographer has made for the positions of the dancers on stage and how they get from one place to another. This may be drawn with chalk on the floor and, even in performance, some of these marks may be seen.

With children, awareness of the design on the floor created by a movement leads to many insights. Does the line on the floor influence the movement of the body? Does the design add to the interest of the dance? Are there other types of learning to be accomplished through study of floor patterns in dance? The following activities focus attention on some of these questions.

❋ A C T I V I T Y 1

Figure Eight

Step 1: Starting at one corner of the room, each child, one at a time, traces the figure eight on the floor. The children may walk or run. They should be encouraged to let their body lean in the direction of the curves as they do it.

Step 2: When the figure has been well established, children draw large figure-eights on a chalkboard or large piece of newsprint paper. They may add colored crayons or chalk to make a design from figure-eights.

See also Appendix: Exercises, Activities, and Themes That Can Be Used to Enhance Learning in Academic Areas, Number Concepts, p. 100.

❀ A C T I V I T Y 2

Letters of the Alphabet

Step 1: The letters of the alphabet may be drawn on the floor with chalk, or large posters, each with a separate letter, may be used. A few letters at a time may be placed on the floor.

Step 2: Children pick a letter they want to use as a floor plan. They may work alone or in pairs. They walk along the lines of the letter they have chosen, using arm and body movements and changing directions as they go. The resultant movement should resemble a short dance.

Step 3: Movements can be done without the letters on the floor. Children may guess what letter is being performed. Several letters might be combined into words or names.

See also Appendix: Exercises, Activities, and Themes That Can Be Used to Enhance Learning in Academic Areas, Language Development, p. 96.

❀ A C T I V I T Y 3

Group Patterns

Starting position: Children stand with partners in each of the four corners of the room. They are numbered 1−2, 3−4, 5−6, 7−8.

Step 1: Partners 1 and 2 with their opposites 5 and 6, skip across the room in eight counts, while 3 and 4 plus 7 and 8 skip in small circles in their corners of the room. The movement is reversed as partners 3 and 4 plus 7 and 8 skip across the room in eight counts, while 1 and 2 plus 5 and 6 skip in small circles.

Step 2: All skip clockwise around the room in the next eight counts.

Step 3: All skip to the center of the room for eight counts, and kneel slowly in four counts. They hold this position. A simple dance has been created with an interesting floor pattern.

❀ A C T I V I T Y 4

Folk Dances

When children can follow directions well enough to perform Activity 3 above, they are ready to do simple folk dances. The various kinds of folk dance contain the directions for floor patterns in their name, for example, round dances, reels, and square dances.

Five- and six-year-olds are able to do a Virginia Reel or a square dance with simple calls. Three- and four-year-olds can do circle games resembling folk dances, such as "Skip to My Lou" or "Hokey Pokey." Here is a good introduction to a circle dance.

Starting position: All join hands and form a circle facing the center. The song to be sung is:

> *Shoo-fly, don't bother me*
> *Shoo-fly, don't bother me*

Shoo-fly, don't bother me
I belong to somebody.

Step 1: On the first line, children walk into the center of the circle. On the second line, they walk backward to their original places. This is repeated on lines three and four.

Step 2: The children then slide around the circle in a clockwise direction as they sing:

I feel, I feel, I feel like a morning star
I feel, I feel, I feel like a morning star

Repeat the dance at a faster tempo. It is important for the children to remember to wait for the beginning of a new phrase before going in or out of the circle. They will sense the structure of a folk dance if they do this, and also recognize the parts A and B of the dance.

See also Appendix: Exercises, Activities, and Themes That Can Be Used to Enhance Learning in Academic Areas, Number Concepts, p. 100.

❀ A C T I V I T Y 5

Creating a Design

Step 1: Children are given large pieces of drawing paper and crayons to create a line drawing using one color and making a continuous line.

Step 2: Children walk the pattern of their design on the floor. They may carry the paper with them.

Step 3: When the design is firmly established, they may walk without the paper, adding arm movements and/or varying the type of locomotor movement.

Step 4: A design can be created using more than one color. Two or three children can walk the floor pattern, each following one of the colored lines. The child who created the pattern to be walked chooses one or two others with whom to work it out.

Step 5: Children take turns showing their designs and moving, using them as floor patterns. Others in the class comment on the design and how effective it was as a floor pattern.

See also Appendix: Exercises, Activities, and Themes That Can Be Used to Enhance Learning in Academic Areas, Art Experiences. p. 103.

Design in all its forms, that is, floor pattern, body shape, and the use of levels and direction, adds to the aesthetic aspects of movement. When children become aware of these elements, they are more sensitive to the meaning of dance. They also have a better background for understanding music through rhythmic experiences and art through space awareness.

Notes

1. Lydia A Gerhardt, *Moving and Knowing* (Englewood Cliffs, N.J.: Prentice Hall, 1973), p. 15.

6

QUALITIES OF MOVEMENT

The quality of movement is the essence of dance. If no feeling, mood, or emotion is evident in the movement, then such movement can be considered exercise. Stretching, bending, swinging, or the locomotor movements of walking, running, leaping, and so forth can be executed as movement experiences but, until some meaning or feeling is instilled into the action, it is not experienced as dance.

People's moods are recognized as much by their movements, their manner of walking and the way they carry their body, as by their facial expression and vocal quality. In every culture, emotion and mood can be interpreted through observing the manner of movement of an individual. Yet it is difficult to identify how these things are sensed.

Laban's Basic Effort Actions

Rudolf von Laban (1879–1958), a dancer and scientist of movement, analyzed the elements that create qualities of movement. Laban found that mood is expressed by particular combinations of the effort elements and the space locations of the movement.

Thus, when a person consciously uses particular combinations of weight, time, and space, he will tend to express a particular mood. In order to be master of his movement, the dancer "must be able to produce the kind of effort mixtures which express any mood demanded of him."[1] Until Laban studied these elements of effort-shape, little was known of the way in which mood is expressed in movement.

In their free dancing, children express mood and feeling without analyzing the particular elements they are incorporating into their movement. Thus, young children are capable of expressive dance when they respond to music, to a story idea, or to some improvisational theme of their own.

Quality of movement should be an essential aspect of teaching dance to young children. With three- through eight-year-olds, qualities are more easily evoked when ideas, music, or themes are used to stimulate responses. Suggestions for such activities, which may or may not relate to the Laban basic effort actions, are given in this chapter. *See also* Appendix: Exercises, Activities, and Themes That Can Be Used to Enhance Learning in Academic Areas, Language Development, p. 97.

However, it is important for teachers of dance for young children to know the properties of the eight basic effort actions described by Laban (see Table 4, and the definitions with suggestions for presentation). In planning a program, whether or not teachers use Laban terminology they should be aware of these effort actions so that children will get the chance to experience all of the eight qualities described by him.

TABLE 4
Properties of the Eight Basic Effort Actions

Action	Time	Weight	Space
Thrusting	Sudden	Firm	Direct
Slashing	Sudden	Firm	Flexible
Floating	Sustained	Fine touch	Flexible
Gliding	Sustained	Fine touch	Direct
Wringing	Sustained	Firm	Flexible
Pressing	Sustained	Firm	Direct
Flicking	Sudden	Fine touch	Flexible
Dabbing	Sudden	Fine touch	Direct

The list of images is adapted from Joan Russel, *Creative Dance in the Primary School* (London: MacDonald & Evans, 1965), pp. 40–41.

In order to understand this table better, it is necessary to know what is meant by the terms "sudden," "sustained," "firm," "fine touch," "direct," and "flexible."[2]

> A sudden movement is sharp, staccato, and can be felt as an immediate discharge of energy. It can be experienced in angular movements with the accompaniment of a sharp beat on drum or rhythm sticks, or with piano chords.
>
> A sustained movement is smooth, slow, and can be felt as a gradual change without interruptions. It can be experienced with legato music or a long, quiet tone on a gong.
>
> A firm movement is strong and forceful and employs the muscular power of the body. It can be experienced in pushing while meeting

resistance. Strong drum beats help children to experience this quality.

A fine touch movement is delicate, light, and buoyant. The body feels as if it is carried by the air. A triangle or bells help children to experience this quality.

A direct movement is straight and moves in a nondeviating path through space. Attention must be focused on the place of arrival.

A flexible movement is wavy and undulating. It wanders through space and several parts of the body may be going in different directions at the same time.

It is advisable to work on pairs of opposites, which helps to clarify meanings and also to relieve tensions through compensatory action.

The eight basic effort actions of Laban can now be explained more fully. Teachers may use the words in the above table to describe time, weight, and space, or they may prefer to evoke these qualities with imagery. Laban's descriptions accurately convey the qualities of movement seen in dance, but his terminology may not be meaningful to young children. Therefore, suggested imagery for each of the eight qualities is included.[3] The qualities are also listed in such an order that they can be experienced as contrasting pairs: thrusting and floating, slashing and gliding, wringing and dabbing, and pressing and flicking.

Thrusting: Can be experienced through stepping, jumping, or galloping with accent into the ground, or by using driving gestures with fists, elbows, feet, or knees. Words like "push," "stamp," or "punch" might create the quality of movement for young children.

Floating: In contrast to thrusting, floating is weightless stirring and turning with many directions for parts of the body. Images of clouds, ripples on water, trees swaying in the wind might evoke the quality.

Slashing: Can be experienced in a whipping action of arms and legs with a curved or scattered pattern. Scissors cutting through paper or some forms of karate movements might evoke the quality.

Gliding: Can be experienced in smoothing gestures, using the palm of the hand to lead the action. It can also be evoked through images of ice skating.

Wringing: Can be experienced in strong turning and twisting with tension in the body. Being the cloth that is wrung out after washing or machinery that screws into wood might be appropriate images.

Dabbing: Contrasts with wringing and is experienced by use of the extremities, in light running, tapping with the feet, or in quick darting movements of the hands or feet. The image of using a paint brush to make bright splashes on a paper on an easel might be helpful.

Pressing: Can best be experienced in the pressure of one hand against the other or of the feet against the floor. The image of pressing clay before molding it can be used.

Flicking: Can be experienced by moving fingers and wrists in a quick, lively, roundabout way, in light turns and leaps, and scattering gestures. Autumn leaves blowing in the wind might be a good image.

To clarify or intensify the desired movement quality, teachers might speak of sudden or smooth movements, using strong or delicate movements, or moving in straight or curvy lines. Other ways to evoke different qualities of movement are discussed in the following sections.

Language-Evoked

Descriptive words are perhaps the best way to evoke qualities of movement. Laban's eight basic effort actions are descriptive words, although some of them might not be familiar to a young child.

Teachers should be aware of the language of children, so that meaningful words can be used, such as "squiggly," "mushy," or "squishy." Children sometimes make up their own words, and they should be encouraged to do this. A question like *How does that word make you feel?* and then *Can you move the way it makes you feel?* can lead to some imaginative verbal expression as well as interesting movement.

Jack Wiener, working with children at the Queens (New York) Youth Center for the Arts, used words like "clay" for heaviness, "wire" for hardness, "rubber band" for lightness, and "piano" for softness. His children responded with imaginative images and exciting movement patterns. Their concentration and intensity were evident in a series of pictures included in his book.[4] But the words themselves were not enough to stimulate such intense response. The teacher's involvement and total empathy with the children's feelings played a great part. Wiener says, "The teacher . . . needs word images to help children identify with the qualities and to give connected wholeness to their expression"[5]

✿ A C T I V I T Y 1

Descriptive Words

Step 1: The teacher lists words on a blackboard or poster paper and reads them to the class. They discuss how these words make them feel. Some suggestions:

funny	ashamed	hungry	disgusted
angry	lazy	soft	bumpy
thoughtful	sleepy	wrinkly	sad
scared	asleep	excited	happy
scary	afraid	wild	surprised

Step 2: Each child picks a word to "act out." The children move, but do not speak, the way the word makes them feel. Word meanings can be clarified.

(Is "scary" the same as "scared"? Is "asleep" the same as "sleeping"? Do "surprised" and "excited" have the same meaning?)

Children often do not understand the difference between similar words until they are asked to "act them out." A feeling response can be stimulated, (*Think of a time when you felt this way.*)

Step 3: The class is asked to guess which word the performer has selected. The person who guesses then has a turn to pick a word to "act out."

Step 4: Children can be divided into two groups. Each group makes up a word or group of words to act out while the other group guesses what they are enacting. This is the well-known "charade" game. Young children need adult assistance to play it.

See also Appendix: Exercises, Activities, and Themes That Can Be Used to Enhance Learning in Academic Areas, Language Development, p. 97.

❀ A C T I V I T Y 2

"Walk as if..."

Step 1: Children stand in a circle facing the line of direction. Walk in time to a drum beat, then take heavy steps as the drum becomes louder and slower. (*How does that make you feel? Who might walk like that?*) The children might respond with "a giant" or "a monster." The teacher encourages responses and elaborates them. (*Walk as if you were that person.*)

Step 2: Teacher plays light, fast beats on a triangle or rim of the drum. She asks the same questions. Children may respond with "a fairy" or "a butterfly." Teacher elaborates. (*Move as if you were that thing.*)

Step 3: (*Walk as if you are a proud prince or princess. You must stand up tall, head high, and feel very elegant and proud.*) A balletic walk with toes coming down before heels might be suggested. (*Now you are a prince or princess in a ballet story like "Cinderella" or "The Nutcracker."*)

Step 4: (*Can you walk as if you are feeling afraid?*) Instinctively, the children contract in the middle, shoulders hunched forward. (*Good. Now try walking backward, as if you are drawing away from something scary.*)

Step 5: (*Let's try a happy walk. Imagine that you are on your way to a carnival, or someplace else you really enjoy.*) Many children will start skipping or bouncing along (see Open-Ended Stories: "The Scarecrow," p. 88.).

Step 6: (*Let's do a sad walk. Think about something sad. Perhaps you just found out that your best friend is moving away.*) Children respond with slower walk, head down.

Step 7: (*Let's see how you walk when you are feeling angry.*) Loud, percussive sounds accompany movement. Children use stamps, some kick the ground as they walk.

See also Appendix: Exercises, Activities, and Themes That Can Be Used to Enhance Learning in Academic Areas, Language Development, p. 97.

TABLE 5

Suggested Music for Specific Emotional Content

Emotion	Composer	Piece
Happiness/Joy	Gershwin	*An American in Paris*
	Handel	*Messiah*
	Mendelssohn	*A Midsummer Night's Dream*
	Mozart	*German Dances*
	Sousa	*Washington Post March*
	Tchaikovsky	*Waltz of the Flowers*
Anger	Chopin	*Polonaise:* A-flat Major,
		Etude: G-flat Major
	Dukas	*The Sorcerer's Apprentice*
	Rachmaninoff	*Piano Concerto no. 1*
	Wagner	*Die Walküre*
Fear	Holst	*The Planets: Mars, Bringer of War*
	Moussorgsky	*Night on Bald Mountain*
	Tibetan Chant	*Lament for the Dead*
Sadness	Brahms	*Piano Concerto no. 2 (2nd Movement)*
	Debussy	*Beau Soir*
		Three Nocturnes
	Ravel	*Le Tombeau de Couperin*
	Wagner	*Tristan and Isolde: Liebestod*
Excitement	Berlioz	*Symphonie Fantastique*
	De Falla	*Ritual Fire Dance*
	Stravinsky	*Firebird Suite*

This list is by no means exhaustive or absolute. Once children become familiar with exploring various emotional content in music, they can start adding to the collection themselves.

From Diane Lynch Fraser, *Playdancing: Discovering and Developing Creativity in Young Children* (Pennington, NJ: Princeton Book Company, Publishers, 1991), p. 63.

❁ A C T I V I T Y 3

Poems

Step 1: Moving to poetry has particular appeal to young children. They respond both to the rhythm of the poem and to the quality suggested by the words. In previous chapters, nursery rhymes have been used to develop rhythmic patterns, and the poem "The Swing" was used to give quality to swinging movements.

Many poems for children are suitable for movement interpretation. Those with onomatopoeia—words whose sounds suggest their meaning—are particularly desirable because the sounds help to develop the quality of movement. One such poem is "Autumn Leaves."[6]

> *Down, down, down*
> > *Red, yellow, brown*
> *Autumn leaves tumble down*
> > *Autumn leaves crumble down*
> *Autumn leaves bumble down*
> > *Flaking and shaking*
> *Tumble down leaves.*

> *Skittery*
> > *Flittery*
> *Rustle by*
> > *Hustle by*
> *Crackle and crunch*
> > *In a snappety bunch.*

> *Run and catch*
> > *Run and snatch*
> *Butterfly leaves*
> > *Sailboat leaves*
> *Windstorm leaves.*

> > *Can you catch them?*

> *Swoop*
> > *Scoop*
> *Pile them up in a stumpy pile and*
> > *Jump*
> *Jump*
> > *Jump!*

Step 1: The poem is read to the children. They are asked to talk about the words that reminded them of personal experiences. For example, the word "crunch" has a sound that suggests "eating cereal" to many children.

Step 2: The children are asked to move to individual words in the poem, such as "skittery" and "flittery," followed by "rustle by" and "hustle by." (*The first two words are fast and light, aren't they?*) The next sounds seem slower and longer. The words "butterfly," "sailboat," and "windstorm" are discussed and children make associations with them. (*These are different ways that leaves fall down. Can you show me?*)

Step 3: Children act out the poem as the teacher recites it, giving emphasis to some words and changing tempo at times as the teacher sees fit.

Step 4: Children are selected to do separate parts of the poem. Some may be "butterfly leaves," some may be "sailboat leaves," some may be "windstorm leaves." The difference in quality of movement can be stressed. (*"Butterfly"* suggests fluttering, doesn't it? And "sailboats" might be floating. How do you think "windstorm leaves" would move?)

Step 5: Children are asked to bring in a favorite poem for "acting out." Poems about animals are favorites, and the words and rhythm of these poems often suggest the movement quality of the animals described. Two examples are "Mice," by Rose Fyleman, and "The Little Turtle," by Vachel Lindsay.[7]

See also Appendix: Exercises, Activities, and Themes That Can Be Used to Enhance Learning in Academic Areas, Language Development, p. 97.

Art-Evoked

Artists work with color, line, and shape to create emotional qualities. When people view a painting, they do not always sense why it gives them a special feeling. But a work of art has significant form in which patterns evolve and contrast with each other to communicate with the viewer.

Every artist knows that certain colors evoke certain feelings, that lines and shapes as well as the subject matter of the picture influence thought. Whistler's famous painting of his mother is called *Arrangement in Gray, No. 1,* and it is the shades of color and the curved shapes that give the feeling of serenity.

Response to color is instinctive and, just as body movement conveys emotions, colors produce certain feelings. It is hard to explain why this is so but the universality of responses to color tend to justify this claim. Lines and shapes also evoke feelings. These instinctive responses are called on to evoke qualities in movement.

❀ A C T I V I T Y 1

Working with Colors

Step 1: Children are shown colored scarves and are asked about them. (*How does this color make you feel? What does this color suggest to you?*) Children usually respond quickly, some with descriptions of feelings and others with associations made with the color: "Red makes me feel happy" or "Red makes me feel like a queen."

Step 2: Scarves are given out. An attempt should be made to give the color to the child who responded strongly to that color when the scarves were shown to the class.

Step 3: Children take turns moving with their colored scarves. Suitable music might be played (see Table 5, p. 74, for suggestions) when the feeling the child wants to express is known.

Step 4: A group improvisation might be developed. One suggestion is that a magician with a black scarf stirs up a mysterious brew. He casts a spell on the other children holding different colored scarves. The "colors" then become alive and dance with the scarf, expressing the feeling of their particular color.

See also Appendix: Exercises, Activities, and Themes That Can Be Used to

Enhance Learning in Academic Areas, Art Experiences, p. 103.

❀ A C T I V I T Y 2

Working with Lines

Step 1: Lines for use as floor patterns have been described in the previous chapter. In this activity, the teacher draws lines on a blackboard or on a transparent plastic to be shown on an overhead projector, such as

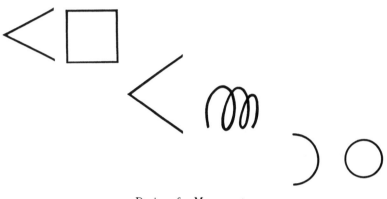

Designs for Movement

Children are asked how these lines make them feel.

Step 2: Teacher opens a discussion (*Look at the lines that go this way* [pointing to vertical lines], *and look at those that go this way* [pointing to horizontal lines]. *Which one would be more exciting?* There is usually general agreement that vertical lines are more exciting. (*Actors and dancers use these lines as floor patterns and the direction of their movement on stage tells something about the feeling of the dance or about the character in a play.*)

Step 3: Each child chooses one of the line designs to interpret in movement— as a floor pattern, as a shape taken by the body, or simply as the feeling the line evokes.

Step 4: The class is divided into small groups. Each group uses one or two of the line designs to create patterns in space.

See also Appendix: Exercises, Activities, and Themes That Can Be Used to Enhance Learning in Academic Areas, Art Experiences, p. 103.

❀ A C T I V I T Y 3

Interpreting Paintings

Step 1: Prints of famous paintings are shown to the class. Children are asked to tell how the paintings make them feel. Van Gogh's *Starry Night* usually evokes a strong response. (*Can you see some rhythm in this painting?*)

Step 2: Children are asked to move to the way the painting makes them feel, and to accompany themselves with humming or whistling sounds.

Step 3: Children discuss what they feel and what they think the artist was feeling. (*There are stars, and the artist is excited by them. Some are big, swirly movements and others are smaller. Can you do circular movements with your hands? With your arms? With your whole body? Some are fast and some are slower. Can you feel the excitment?*)

Step 4: Children are shown other paintings by Van Gogh. They are asked to make drawings about any subject, using lines, rhythm, and colors to add to the excitement.

See also Appendix: Exercises, Activities, and Themes That Can Be Used to Enhance Learning in Academic Areas, Art Experiences, p. 103.

❀ A C T I V I T Y 4

Interpreting Sculpture

Step 1: Pictures of well-known sculpture are shown to the class. Some suggestions are Arp's *Venus of Meudon* and *Ptolemy*, or Rodin's *Woman in Marble* and *The Cathedral*.

Step 2: Teacher suggests movement. (*Can you move the way the sculpture makes you feel? You may start with the position of the sculpture and move from there.*)

Step 3: The children are given some clay and are directed to see what kinds of shapes it makes.

See also Appendix: Exercises, Activities, and Themes That Can Be Used to Enhance Learning in Academic Areas, Art Experiences, p. 103.

Music-Evoked

Music is the universal language that can soothe, excite, stimulate, or relax the listener. Music is used to arouse groups, as in marching music. It is used as lullabies to quiet babies. It evokes feelings of love, as in every kind of popular ballad or operatic aria. In every culture, music is an essential part of ceremonials, to unite groups in prayer or to commemorate important life moments such as birth, marriage, or death.

With young children, music often accompanies movement. They chant as they skip, they hum as they swing their arms. Dance classes traditionally have the accompaniment of a piano, a drum, or records. In this section the use of music to heighten movement quality is emphasized.

❀ A C T I V I T Y 1

Qualities of Sound in Rhythm Instruments

Activities using rhythm instruments were presented in Chapter 4. Here, the tone quality of each rhythm instrument is considered.

Step 1: Children sit in a semicircle on the floor. Teacher sits facing them, with several instruments on the floor beside her. (*I want to talk to you a few minutes about the different sounds the instruments make. Do they all sound alike?*)

Step 2: Teacher plays a triangle, then maracas. (*How are these two instruments different? Which sound lasts longer?*) Children discover that the rattle stops fast but the triangle dies away. Teacher continues to try different instruments— hand drum, tom-tom, tambourine, cymbal, rhythm sticks. Children are asked to describe and compare the sounds that they hear.

Step 3: Instruments are distributed, one to every two children. Working with partners, they take turns accompanying each other's movement. The emphasis is on interpreting the quality of the sound made by the different instruments.

Step 4: Some children may prefer to accompany themselves as they move. For example, a child may use a tambourine, shaking it as she turns, hitting it with her hand as she jumps.

Step 5: Each child, or each pair of partners, shows the rest of the class what they have done. Children evaluate each other, both on the way the movement reflected the quality of the sound and on how well the rhythm accompanied the movement.

✤ A C T I V I T Y 2

Theme and Variation

Step 1: Children listen to a piano piece[8] in which "Three Blind Mice" is played with several variations. (*Even though the melody is the same, there are different ways it is played.*) Children are asked to tell the differences they hear. They may note that one section is fast and bouncy, another is slower and may sound sad (one variation is in a minor key).

Step 2: Children move around the room, changing the quality of their movement as the music changes.

✤ A C T I V I T Y 3

Interpreting Musical Selections

Step 1: Three selections of music,[9] having very different qualities, are played to the class: "Fountain Dance," from *Wand of Youth No. 2,* by Elgar; "Bydlo," from *Pictures at an Exhibition,* by Moussorgsky; "Departure," from *Winter Holiday,* by Prokofiev.

Step 2: Children are not told the titles of the music. They are asked to tell about what they hear. Although the images may be quite different, the feeling tone usually corresponds to the quality of the orchestral pieces. Some responses might be: for "Fountain Dance"—fairies, leprechauns, butterflies; for "Bydlo"—a giant crying, an ox pulling something heavy; for "Departure"— catching a train, galloping on horse, an auto race.

Step 3: Children are asked to "act out" the images they have envisioned.

Step 4: A few images are selected and several children are assigned to groups to work on each one. Each group then presents its interpretation to the class. (*How close does this interpretation come to the feeling of the music?*)

Qualities of movement are evoked from improvisational themes and stories for dramatization presented to the class. These are worked on over a period of time and may become end-term demonstrations. Examples of such themes are presented in the next chapter.

Notes

1. Valerie Preston-Dunlop, *A Handbook for Modern Educational Dance.* 2d ed. (Boston: Plays, 1980), p. 138.
2. The list of images is adapted from Joan Russell, *Creative Dance in the Primary School* (London: MacDonald & Evans, 1965), pp. 40–41.
3. The six movement descriptions are adapted from Preston-Dunlop, p. 48.
4. Jack Wiener, *Creative Movement for Children* (New York: Van Nostrand Reinhold, 1969).
5. *Ibid.,* p. 38.
6. From Eve Merriam, *There's No Rhyme for Silver* (New York: Atheneum, 1962).
7. Both poems are in Helen and Harry Heltman (eds.), *Let's Read Together Poems* (New York: Row, Peterson, 1949).
8. John Thompson, *Variations on the Theme "Three Blind Mice."* Students' Series for the Piano (Cincinnati: Willis Music Co., n.d.).
9. All the selections are on *Adventures in Music,* selected by Gladys Tipton. RCA Victor LE1001, Grade 2.

7

THEMES FOR IMPROVISATION

With young children, stories are motivation for creativity. They love to "act out" familiar fairy tales and, someplace along the way, these ideas can be developed into simple group dances. The teacher may act as narrator. Appropriate musical accompaniment may be used, but the teacher's drum or use of the voice is usually sufficient to hold the group together.

Stories are frequently found on children's records or cassette tapes. These may provide interesting ideas to begin with, but rarely are they suitable for dance accompaniment. The action is narrated too quickly to develop movement sequences. The stories may be listened to, and then retold by the teacher at a pace that is suited to the children's ideas in movement.

Many of the themes described below are classic folk tales. Others are open-ended stories that the children's improvisations in movement will complete. Finally, there is a section suggesting long-term projects that might be used for end-of-term demonstrations.

All of these are suggestions and can be expanded or reduced to fit the needs of the class. Other themes might develop from classroom activity. They might evolve from studies of different cultures or from favorite selections of literature. Children might also be invited to bring in favorite stories or poems that they would like to develop into dances.

Classic Tales

In Chapter 4 the use of nursery rhymes and some classic stories was mentioned: the image of Jack running away from the Giant was useful in establishing the contrast between slow, heavy walks and light running steps; "The Three Bears" and "Three Billy Goats Gruff" demonstrated changes in tempo and dynamics as they were acted out.

Nursery rhymes, such as "Little Miss Muffet," have been used to emphasize rhythmic pattern and phrasing. Any of these ideas can be developed into improvisational dances. Individual children, partners, or small groups can prepare a dance to show to the class.

In the following selections suggestions are made for those sections of the classic tales that have been most successfully made into dance improvisations. The children should be familiar with the entire story, but for the purpose of developing a dance only certain scenes will be appropriate. The teacher or an older child might narrate the story and introduce the scenes to be danced.

✿ T H E M E 1

"Jack and the Beanstalk"

This story is modified to emphasize the action and to minimize the frightening role of the Giant, who "smells the blood of an Englishman!" He simply says, "Fee, Fi, Fo, Fum—I am a Giant and here I come!" The scenes that lend themselves to dance improvisation are enacted by the whole class; later, parts may be assigned.

Step 1: Jack plants the colored beans in the ground. Children then squat down and become the beans. They grow out of the ground and become the beanstalk that reaches up to the sky. Then they all become Jack and develop movement that suggests they are climbing the beanstalk.

Step 2: All the children reach the "sky" and begin to walk on clouds. (*Feel the clouds all around you. You must walk very lightly, on tip-toe.*)

Step 3: Children see a castle and walk up to it very cautiously. They knock on the door.

Step 4: All of them now become the Giant, who takes big, heavy steps. Jack runs with light tiptoe steps, twice as fast as the Giant's rhythm. Children alternate between moving like the Giant and being Jack. (The teacher may alternate beats on the drum with light, fast beats on the drum rim or on a triangle.)

Step 5: All the children, as Jack, climb down the beanstalk, get a hatchet, and chop down the beanstalk.

This story has great appeal and is remembered by very young children, who can retell it in sequence once they have acted it out.

See also Appendix: Exercises, Activities, and Themes That Can Be Used to Enhance Learning in Academic Areas, Language Development; Exploring Science; Art Experiences, pp. 97; 102; 103.

✿ **T H E M E 2**

"Peter and the Wolf"

The Prokofiev music is narrated on the recording and has been done by many actors; choose one who emphasizes the feeling of the music rather than using inappropriate clowning.

The beginning of the music introduces the characters, using selected instruments of the orchestra to represent them. Much time should be spent on this part so that the children recognize the musical themes for each character.

Step 1: Whole class moves to the introduction of the characters, successively being the bird, the duck, the cat, Peter, the grandfather, the wolf, and the hunters. Teacher should look for those children who most effectively represent the characters, so that they may be selected later to enact the story.

Step 2: Working in pairs, children improvise the argument between the bird and the duck. They alternate movements, the child playing the bird moving on "What kind of a duck are you if you can't fly?" and the child being the duck moving on "What kind of a bird are you if you can't swim?"

Step 3: Cat movements can be done by all of the children, and then one might be chosen to sneak up on the duck and bird who are still arguing.

Step 4: All can improvise movements of the wolf as he is being caught. (*Try to get away, but the rope is around your tail and you can't get loose.*)

Step 5: After segments of the story have been improvised, selection is made for children to play various parts. The recording is then played, but may have to be edited to shorten it.

Step 6: Remaining children enter as hunters and lead the rest of the cast to the zoo.

This is a well-loved story that has action and excitement with which the children can identify. It is particularly good for developing animal movements, emphasizing the differences among them.

See also Appendix: Exercises, Activities, and Themes That Can Be Used to Enhance Learning in Academic Areas, Language Development; Exploring Science; Art Experiences, Experiencing Music. pp. 97; 102; 103; 105.

✿ **T H E M E 3**

"Hansel and Gretel"

Selections from Humperdinck's famous opera can be used to accompany the following scenes:

Step 1: Children take partners, becoming Hansel or Gretel. All of them pantomime making brooms, but tiring of work they stop to play and dance:

> *Brother, come and dance with me,*
> *Both my hands I offer thee,*
> *Right foot first, left foot then,*
> *Round about and back again.*

Action should follow words of the song, turning in a circle on the last line.

Step 2: Children are taken to the woods, where they become lost. Movement improvisation is done to feelings of being lost in the woods, and eventually becoming tired and lying down to sleep (music for "When at night I go to sleep/Fourteen angels watch will keep" can be used).

Step 3: Children awaken and see the candy house. They approach it cautiously.

Step 4: All the children may then move like witches coming out of the candy house, enticing Hansel and Gretel to come in.

This story is particularly appropriate for developing awareness of mood and quality of movement. It includes happy play, feelings of being lost, surprise, excitement, and fear—all of which can be expressed in movement.

See also Appendix: Exercises, Activities, and Themes That Can Be Used to Enhance Learning in Academic Areas, Language Development; Art Experiences, Experiencing Music. pp. 97; 103; 105-106.

❀ T H E M E 4

"Cinderella"

The Prokofiev ballet music has some fine sections for dance accompaniment. The following scenes are good for improvisation.

Step 1: The ugly stepsisters argue and give orders to Cinderella. The suggested music is percussive and encourages children to do sharp, angular movements. The class might be divided into trios, two sisters and Cinderella, as they enlarge the pantomime of bickering into dance.

Step 2: When Cinderella is alone, the Fairy Godmother appears. A duet between Cinderella and the Fairy Godmother can be developed. Pairs of children can improvise to an appropriate section of the ballet music, which is lyrical. At the end of the duet, Cinderella is transformed from her ugly appearance to beauty. The pair dance together.

Step 3: Everyone rejoices at the wedding. A more formal dance, in promenade formation, might be introduced here for older groups.

Although many parts of the story need to be narrated, the selected sections offer opportunities to develop dances through improvisation and/or simple choreography.

See also Appendix: Exercises, Activities, and Themes That Can Be Used to Enhance Learning in Academic Areas, Language Development; Art Experiences, Experiencing Music. pp. 97; 103; 106.

Open-Ended Stories

These are stories begun by the teacher but completed by the class. Each child may add one part or the group may decide how the story is to end before they act it out.

It is difficult to give sources for these stories because they have evolved in class over many years and the endings are never quite the same. Some of them may have originated from an idea on a children's record or picture storybook. Many were suggestions brought into class by children. All of the stories have been successful in giving impetus to dance.

Can You Rock Like A Rocking Horse?

❀ T H E M E 1

"The Little Rocking Horse"

Some groups of children may not be familiar with rocking horses. A toy model or a picture should be presented by the teacher as she begins the story.

Step 1: A little rocking horse, named Rocky, is in a toy store where all he can do is rock and rock all day long. (*Can you show me how you can rock? You may sit or stand. You may lie on your back or on your stomach. Yes, good. Now, find another way to rock. Here is a song to rock to.*)

> *I'm rocking, rocking all the time,*
> *I wish that I could move,*
> *I'm rocking, rocking all the time,*
> *In the same old groove.*
>
> *I wish that I could go someplace,*
> *I'd like to run away,*
> *But here I always have to stay,*
> *And rock and rock all day.*

Step 2: (*Rocky rocks harder and harder on his rockers and finally he rocks so hard that he jumps off the rockers and gallops away.*) Children gallop around the room in time to the teacher's uneven rhythm on the drum.

Step 3: Rocky meets a policeman (the teacher). (*Stop!* Holds up hand. *Where are you going, little rocking horse?*) Children answer that they are running away; they want to be real live horses (or other reasons).

The policeman answers. (*Do you think I can ride on your back? Some policemen ride horses, you know.*) Children pretend to be policemen's horses, raising knees high off the ground and with heads held high proudly. (*People laugh at a big policeman riding on a toy horse! You are not big enough to be a policeman's horse, Rocky. There is a circus just outside town. Why don't you see if they can use you there?*) Children gallop off to the circus.

Step 4: At the circus, Rocky tries to be a circus horse, with a bareback rider on his back. The children alternate between slow trots of a circus horse and the bareback rider standing on his back with one leg raised behind him. The change from trotting to a still, arabesque position is very good for developing a sense of balance. But the circus man refuses to have Rocky. (*You can't be a circus horse, Rocky. You don't ride smoothly enough. The bareback rider will fall off your back.*) So Rocky gallops off to visit another place.

Step 5: Children suggest where Rocky might go next, for example, (1) the farm—Rocky tries to pull a wagon. He is not strong enough; (2) the racetrack—Rocky does not run fast enough; (3) the rodeo—The cowboys try to ride him as they lasso some steer, but Rocky is not brave enough and is frightened by the animals.

Other suggestions are possible as the children make their own contributions. These are only a few ideas that have been used.

Step 6: Finally, Rocky decides to go back to the toy store, where he jumps on his rockers and begins rocking again.

> *I'm rocking, rocking all the time,*
> *I don't want to run away,*
> *I'm rocking, rocking all the time,*
> *And here I want to stay.*
>
> *I thought I'd like to go someplace,*
> *I wanted to run away,*
> *But here I always want to stay,*
> *And rock and rock all day.*

This story not only develops imagination and variety in movement but is an excellent way to enrich vocabulary. Equivalents like "not big enough" is "too little;" "not brave enough" is "afraid;" not smooth enough" is "bumpy;" "not strong enough" is "too weak" can be stressed.

See also Appendix: Exercises, Activities, and Themes That Can Be Used to Enhance Learning in Academic Areas, Language Development; Social Learning; Art Experiences. pp. 97; 101; 103.

❁ T H E M E   2

"A Day in the Park"

Step 1: Children come to the park to play. They come through a gate, one at a time. The teacher can be the gatekeeper, or even the rotating turnstile. She can assign children to an area where they can play—some to the swings, some on seesaws, some on the jungle gym. Children improvise movements in time to a beat or to some selected music.

Step 2: As they continue to play, other children enter as characters you might meet in the park: a lady with a baby carriage, an old man, and so forth. A policeman might help a lost boy to find his mother, a girl might be looking for a friend who does not come. Various situations can be invented by the children.

Step 3: A rainstorm sends all the people in the park rushing for cover. Teacher designates a place in the room that will be an imaginary shed. (The music "Golliwogg's Cakewalk" from Debussy's *Children's Corner Suite* seems to make a natural accompaniment for this action.)

See also Appendix: Exercises, Activities, and Themes That Can Be Used to Enhance Learning in Academic Areas, Language Development; Art Experiences, Experiencing Music. pp. 97; 103; 106.

Theme 3

"Halloween"

This is a favorite holiday for young children and they love to act out scary creatures associated with it. The following are ones that lend themselves to dance improvisations.

Step 1: Cats—*Let's all get on our knees. Round your backs like angry cats. Now, as you arch your back, pick up your head and make a hissing sound* (see Exercise 2 of Body Alignment, p. 15).

Step 2: Ghosts—*Let's float around the room like clouds. Ghosts move in wavy patterns. You are not sure where their arms are. Float like a ghost.* (A gong or triangle can be used for accompaniment.

Step 3: Skeletons—*Your bones rattle as you walk. Your movements are sharp and angular.* (Sticks can be hit together to make a sharp, percussive sound.)

Step 4: Witches—*Let's get on our broomsticks and gallop around the room.* An uneven beat on a drum can accompany this.)

Step 5: The class is divided into four groups—cats, ghosts, skeletons, and witches. Each group is sent to a corner of the room. The music, *Danse Macabre* by Saint Saëns, is played. It begins with twelve chimes denoting midnight. Each group enters on a different section of the music, performs its movements, and returns to its corner. When the clock chimes again, all the children lie down and stop moving. The macabre dancers are gone and will not appear again until next Halloween.

See also Appendix: Exercises, Activities, and Themes That Can Be Used to Enhance Learning in Academic Areas, Language Development; Art Experiences; Experiencing Music, pp. 97; 103; 106.

✿ THEME 4

"The Toy Store"

The children decide what toy they want to be—train, car, soldier, ballerina doll, mechanical animal, Superman, and so forth. They are placed around the room and "freeze" in characteristic positions.

Step 1: A child selected to be the storekeeper adjusts some of the "toys" and dusts them off. A child selected to be a customer enters. The storekeeper shows her one toy at a time and each one demonstrates what he can do. The customer does not buy anything.

Step 2: The storekeeper displays a sign, "SALE." *The toys don't want to be sold and separated from their friends. At midnight they come alive and dance with each other. They decide to pretend they are broken, so they will not be sold.* (This part can be narrated by the teacher.)

Step 3: Each of the toys moves as if it were broken. The next morning, the storekeeper tries one at a time and is angry that they do not work right. He decides to send them to the Salvation Army for repair. The toys are happy because they can stay together.

A similar version of this story can be done at Christmas time, with Santa Claus substituted for the storekeeper. Suitable music might be the music of the Act 2 grand pas de deux of the Sugar-Plum Fairy from Tchaikovsky's *Nutcracker* and "Jingle Bells" for parts of the Santa Claus version. Santa's helpers might fix the toys that are broken so that they can be delivered to children. Each child then plays and dances with the toy of choice.

See also Appendix: Exercises, Activities, and Themes That Can Be Used to Enhance Learning in Academic Areas, Language Development; Social Learning; Art Experiences. pp. 97; 101; 103.

✿ THEME 5

"The Scarecrow"

Step 1: *A boy wants to go to a fair, but his mother will not allow him to go. He decides to run away, but he gets lost in the woods on the way. He falls asleep, and a witch, who knows he is being bad, casts a spell on him. When he awakens, he is stiff and unable to move. He is a scarecrow.* Children can pantomine this action and then can try to move as a scarecrow might.

Step 2: Various people then pass through the woods on the way to the fair. They are suprised to see a scarecrow in the woods, and each reacts differently. Children should invent their own characters and, one or two at a time, they approach the scarecrow. Some suggestions are a clown who works at the fair, two playful boys who tease the scarecrow, a lonesome girl who tries to be friends with him, the mother of the boy and who became a scarecrow and who is looking for him.

Step 3: The end of the story can be created by the children as well but, somehow or other, the scarecrow becomes a little boy again.

See also Appendix: Exercises, Activities, and Themes That Can Be Used to Enhance Learning in Academic Areas, Language Development; Art Experiences. pp. 97; 103.

Themes for Long-Term Projects

Sometimes a class is ready to work on a long-term project that might be extended over several class periods. Such projects might be divided into sections so that each classtime is devoted to one of them.

Beginning with improvisations, some parts of these dances might be set by the teacher to form simple choreography. An end-term demonstration, to which parents are invited, might result.

❁ T H E M E 1

"The Seasons"

At four consecutive sessions, the children discuss what occurs in the four seasons of the year. They may talk about various weather conditions, the activities with which they are involved, the holidays that occur at each season, and so forth. The class is then divided into small groups. Each group chooses one of the ideas and works it out in movement. The groups then present their improvisations to the rest of the class. The following are some suggestions.

Spring: Flowers growing, April showers, winds blowing, baseball. An anonymous poem that might be used here is especially effective with three- and four-year-olds:

> *In the heart of a seed,*
> > *Buried deep, so deep;*
> > *A dear little seed,*
> *Lay fast asleep.*
>
> *"Wake," said the sunshine,*
> > *"And turn to the light;"*
> *"Wake," said the voice of the raindrops bright.*
>
> *The little seed heard,*
> > *And it rose to see,*
> *What the wonderful outside world might be!*

Summer: Going to the beach, playing in the playground, camping, ocean waves, climbing mountains, wading in streams, fishing. Edith Segal's poem, "The Forever Sea," lends itself to dramatization:

> *I love to go down to the sandy shore,*
> > *And watch the forever sea;*

The waves roll high into big white curls,
Then unroll and race toward me.

One morning I counted up to ten,
I counted to twenty-three;
Still the waves rolled high into big white curls,
Then unrolled and raced toward me.

And if I could stay on the sandy shore,
And count to a million-and-three,
The waves would still roll into big white curls,
Then unroll and race toward me.

The waves have been rolling so very long,
Before there was you or me;
Yes, I love to go down to the sandy shore,
And watch the FOREVER SEA.[1]

Autumn: Leaves falling, raking leaves, football, school begins, Halloween. A lovely poem for movement is Eve Merriam's "Autumn Leaves" (see p. 75).
Winter: Snowflakes, ice skating, snowball fights, skiing, Christmas. A poem by Edith Segal, "Snowflakes," is appropriate:

The lamp hangs high in the cold city streets,
The snowflakes dance by on invisible feet,
They sparkle and twirl in a moment of light,
And on they whirl in the darkness of night.[2]

Poems have been chosen to accompany movement for this theme on "The Seasons." There are many other suitable poems as well as music that might fit each chosen activity. The children or the teacher might have suggestions to make. Those offered here are simply examples.

When all four seasons have been explored and dances improvised about them, a presentation might be prepared. The children can decide which activities are best suited for the theme and were best developed by a group. After selections have been made, each "season" is sent off to a corner of the room. A dancer is selected to visit each of the seasons. As he does so, the scene portraying that season is enacted.

See also Appendix: Exercises, Activities, and Themes That Can Be Used to Enhance Learning in Academic Areas, Language Development; Exploring Science; Art Experiences. pp. 98; 102; 104.

❀ T H E M E   2

"Under the Sea"

The class discusses what it would be like under the sea, how animals and plants move in water, and the colors and shapes of sea life. Pictures from books are shown to them. The music, Debussy's *La Mer* (The Sea), is played for them. It has three parts: "From Dawn to Noon at Sea," "Gambols of the Waves," and "Dialogue of the Wind and the Sea."

Step 1: Children move as if they are underwater. (*Water is heavier than air, so you have to move more slowly, don't you?*) They try this to the music.

Step 2: Accompanied by the music, children move as if they were plants, swaying in the water.

Step 3: Now they try to move as if they were different kinds of fish. (*Some are big fish that move slowly. Some are small fish that move quickly. Some small fish swim together in "schools." Think of yourself as one special kind of fish.*)

Step 4: (*What else might you find "Under the Sea"? Yes, there might be a large turtle, an octopus, clams. Try being one of these.*)

Step 5: The class is divided into three groups. They pick the section of the music they want to use. Construction paper, crepe paper, crayons, and scissors are made available for their use. Each group tries to create an underwater scene in movement, using whatever props they may need. One group may be plants, another may be fish, and the third may be other underwater creatures.

Step 6: A scuba diver is chosen to visit each group after their movement patterns have been established.

Step 7: The entire piece of music is played as each group moves to one of the three sections of it.

If these improvisations work out well, a mural may be created for backdrop, some costuming effects can be produced with the available materials, and a small production can be developed to show to parents or to other classes.

See also Appendix: Exercises, Activities, and Themes That Can Be Used to Enhance Learning in Academic Areas, Language Development; Exploring Science; Experiencing Music. pp. 98; 102; 106.

❈ T H E M E 3

"The Pied Piper of Hamelin"

This poem by Robert Browning is a great favorite for fifth and sixth graders. To be used as a dance project, older children, or adults should be involved: as the narrator who reads the poem, the Pied Piper, Councilmen, and the Mayor. But there are many sections that could be performed by young children. A final production, using various age levels, is a good experience for all involved. Selections from Bela Bartok's piano piece *For Children* make excellent accompaniment. Each character and each part of the poem can have a corresponding theme in the music.

Only those scenes involving young children are described here.

Step 1: Teacher reads the section of the poem that begins "Rats! They fought the dogs and bit the cats...." Children scurry around the room on all fours, as the rats. Occasionally, they stop and sniff the air, moving their head quickly and jerkily. A signal is given for their entrance and exit (good for three- and four-olds).

Step 2: The children of Hamelin are playing. The Pied Piper comes playing his pipe. Children stop and listen. Eventually, they follow the Piper, doing whatever movements he does. This can be a kind of "follow the leader" activity, with the teacher or an older child as the Pied Piper introducing skip combinations or whatever dance steps the children are ready to do (good for five- and six-year-olds).

Step 3: The townspeople grieve at the loss of the children. Seven- and eight-year-olds can improvise sad movements to a section of Bartok's music that is in the minor key. After each child has invented a "sad" movement, the group stands in a line, as one after another of the "grieving parents" comes forward to do his "sad" movement.

See also Appendix: Exercises, Activities, and Themes That Can Be Used to Enhance Learning in Academic Areas, Language Development; Social Learning; Art Experiences. pp. 98; 101; 103.

A Sad Parent in "The Pied Piper of Hamelin"

This project can become a schoolwide event that can be used for an assembly program or an end-of-term recital. While entrances and exits need to be clearly established, the actual movements of the rats, the children, and the grieving townspeople can still be fairly improvisational.

For young children, learning involved choreography is often inhibiting. The quality of the movement is lost if there is too much memorizing to be done.

the movement is lost if there is too much memorizing to be done.

Final projects have some positive effects, as children love to perform and "show off" what they have accomplished. An informal demonstration is preferable to an elaborate recital. A great deal of rehearsing consumes too much time and frequently creates too much excitement and some anxiety for young children.

Any of the themes in this chapter could be developed into long-range projects. But all of the themes should first be presented as ideas for improvisation. Movements can be set by the teacher based on the children's movement ideas.

An attempt has been made in this chapter and throughout the book to present exercises, activities, and themes in developmental sequence. Those at the beginning of each section are simpler than those at the end. The exercises in Chapters 2 and 3 follow this pattern, although they are grouped primarily into movement categories. The activities dealing with components of dance in Chapters 4, 5, and 6 are also grouped developmentally. In this final chapter, dealing with suitable themes for improvisation, the earlier themes are simpler than those that appear later.

These groupings are not fixed and can be selected by teachers to fit the needs of the individual class of students. Some children at ages four or five have the coordination and maturity of seven- or eight-year-olds. Some of the older groups may be less flexible and are not as free in improvisation as younger groups. Teachers must use their discretion in selecting the most appropriate exercises, activities, and themes to suit their class.

It is my hope that classroom teachers will be able to use movement to enhance all learning. Studio teachers and dance specialists will become aware of the contributions of dance to young children's understanding of all areas of learning.

Notes

1. Edith Segal, *Come with Me: Dance Poems for Young People* (New York: Citadel, 1963), p. 10-11.
2. *Ibid.*, p. 15.

APPENDIX

EXERCISES, ACTIVITIES, AND THEMES THAT CAN BE USED TO ENHANCE LEARNING IN ACADEMIC AREAS

Children assimilate knowledge when they can make the information imparted to them part of themselves by becoming actively involved with it. Movement is a way to reach children, an avenue that intrigues and invites them. Teachers can make constructive use of this innate interest and can let body expression be part of the learning process. Ideas that have been discussed in class take on new meaning when children express them in movement. A story, a science idea, an incident from history may become themes for creative dance. As children work with rhythmic patterns in movement, new understandings of number concepts may evolve. When a unit of study is nearing completion, a culminating program involving the children in movement will help set ideas, and new relationships and insights can be perceived.

The following pages present exercises, activities, and themes that relate to areas of learning. Sections on language development, number concepts, social studies, science, art, and music are included. References are made to sections of the text that describe activities that are relevant to each of these subjects. Hopefully this information will be useful to teachers of prechool, kindergarten, and primary grades. Studio dance teachers and physical educators can find material for their classes that will help them to develop understandings in all areas of learning as well as provide them with themes that are meaningful to their students.

Language Development

Exercise	Relationship to learning	Page
Chapter 2 **Swings** Exercise 1 Imagery	Robert Louis Stevenson's poem "The Swing" has the rhythmic pattern of swinging movement throughout. Children appreciate the poem more after they have moved to it. They become aware of the form of the poem by developing different movements for each stanza.	17-19
Body Isolation: Hands Exercise 1 Step 3	The hand game "Open, shut them" holds the interest of young children who are usually intrigued by finger play. Poem has rhyme and humor. Hand movements are explored.	24
Activity Chapter 4 **Tempo** Step 1	Awareness of meaning of "slow" and "fast" are developed. Very young children often confuse slow and fast with loud and soft. Running fast means getting louder to many of them. Following directions given by a drum is another kind of listening skill.	44
Dynamics Activity 5	Story dramatization of "The Three Bears" or "Three Billy Goats Gruff" shows changes in tempo and dynamics for each of the characters. Understanding of sequence of events is evident after dramatization.	47
Accent Activity 1	"Jack-in-the-Box" is an opportunity to sense accent in poem and in movement.	47-48
Rhythmic Pattern Activity 4	Children sense the rhythmic pattern in nursery rhymes and in speech patterns. They learn about syllables as they count the beats. This helps learning to read.	52
Phrasing Activity 1	Children learn to identify phrase in poem or nursery rhyme. Each line of "Little Miss Muffet" makes up one phrase, each having different actions.	55
Chapter 5 **Floor Pattern** Activity 2 Steps 1–3	Letters of the alphabet are used as floor patterns and children walk along lines drawn on the floor. Kinesthetic learning helps children to distinguish shapes of letters.	67

Exercise	Relationship to learning	Page
Chapter 6 **Laban's Actions**	Understanding of vocabulary in Laban's description of movement qualities, such as "sustained," "sudden," "flexible," may be applied to other uses.	69-72
Language-Evoked Activity 1 Steps 1–4	Acting out words is one way to get to understand meanings. Word lists can be made up of verbs (action words) or adverbs and adjectives (descriptive words). Children can learn differences and then use words they have acted out in sentences.	72-73
Activity 2 Steps 1–7	"Walk as if . . ." helps to define words that have differing movement qualities. Children better understand meanings of "proud," "afraid," "happy," "sad," or "angry." They may be asked to create a story around the characters they have enacted.	73-74
Activity 3 Steps 1–5	The poem "Autumn Leaves" has many onomatopoetic words, which the children can interpret in movement. Quality, rhyme, and rhythm can be better appreciated after moving to parts of the poem.	74-76
Chapter 7 **All Activities**	All of the themes described in Chapter 7 relate to language development. The three categories listed in the left margin below may serve slightly different purposes, but all enhance various kinds of language learning.	81-93
Classic Tales	Activities are described for "Jack and the Beanstalk," "Peter and the Wolf," "Hansel and Gretel," and "Cinderella." These stories should be familiar to all children, but, unfortunately, they have been superseded by television's monsters and supermen. Acting out these classic tales makes them popular again. Discussion of characters, plot, and sequence increases literary appreciation.	81-84
Open-Ended Stories	Each of the stories in this section, "The Little Rocking Horse," "A Day in the Park," "Halloween," "The Toy Store," and "The Scarecrow," provides opportunities for	84-89

Exercise	Relationship to learning	Page
	stretching children's imagination. Movement and perhaps dialogue will be improvised by the children at some point. A creative writing session might follow the movement and dance experience.	
Long-Term Projects	The three samples of long-term projects included here, "The Seasons," "Under the Sea," and "The Pied Piper of Hamelin," demonstrate how an idea from a dance class can be extended to involve several scenes and different groups of performers. An end-term production is satisfying to the children, especially if they had a part in creating it. Each of these themes relates to other areas of learning and may serve as culminating experiences when a unit of study is completed. Many other themes can be developed in this way.	89-93

Number Concepts

Exercise	Relationship to learning	Page
Chapter 2 Body Isolation Hands Exercise 2	Very young children learn to count by counting fingers. "This little piggie" and other finger games provide this opportunity.	25
Exercise 4 Step 2	Drawing a figure-eight in the air adds kinesthetic awareness of shape of eight.	25
Chapter 3 Walks Exercise Step 3	Counting four walks and four tiptoe steps establishes one-to-one correspondence—one step for every count.	30
Runs Exercise Step 2	Learning a waltz is a way of sensing three-step combinations or "three-ness," that is, one heavy and two light steps. If the third beat is accented, the children can learn to count by threes, saying only the accented beat out loud: 1, 2, "3," 4, 5, "6," 7, 8, "9."	31
Jumps Exercise Step 4	Two bounces and a jump creates an awareness of three-ness and can be used to teach 3x table as above.	34

Exercise	Relationship to learning	Page
	steps backward, and two more sliding steps to the other side.	
Floor Pattern All Activities	Group patterns and simple folk dances require careful counting. Concentration is needed to avoid confusion.	66-68

Social Learning

Exercise	Relationship to learning	Page
Chapter 2 **Body Isolation** All Exercises	Bouncing various parts of the body can be done to African drum music. Especially well suited to this is Olatunji's *Drums of Passion* (Nigerian). The children will do isolation movements that resemble African tribal dancing. Pictures can be shown after movement improvisation.	22-23
Chapter 3 **Hops** Exercise Step 3	Improvising different kinds of hops can lead to the creation of an Irish jig. This is a good activity to be done at St. Patrick's day and the relationship of dance to holiday celebration can be discussed.	33-34
Combining Locomotor Movements	All folk dance steps are made up of combinations of basic locomotor movements. Polka, schottische, step-hop, or waltz can be demonstrated to show relationships, and cultures in which these dances occur can be discussed. Some Scandinavian folk dances are relatively simple and can be taught to the children. Folk dances are also discussed on page 67.	40-41
Chapter 4 **Tempo** Activity Steps 2-3	Simulating the movement of trains and airplanes can add to the understanding and enjoyment of a unit on "Transportation."	44-45
Chapter 5 **Relating to Others** Activity 1 Activities 2-4	Many social experiences arise from dance classes. Learning to relate well to each other should be part of a social studies program. "Mirroring" is one activity to develop awareness of another person. Other activities to increase sensitivity to others are on page 46. By moving together a group feeling is established.	65-66
Activity 3 All steps	Movements of a machine are simulated, making children more aware of how machinery in a factory works.	65-66

Exercise	Relationship to learning	Page
Chapter 7 **Open-Ended stories** Theme 1 All steps	The story of the rocking horse that becomes a "real, live horse" provides many opportunities to discuss how horses are used by policemen, farmers, cowboys, and others.	82
Theme 4 Steps 1–3	The theme of a toy store provides the opportunity to discuss how stores function. Questions such as "Why did the storekeeper decide to run a sale?" lead to social learnings.	84
Long-Term Projects Theme 3	The story of "The Pied Piper of Hamelin" provides opportunities to discuss how a town council works, the mayor's role, and what may happen when a contract is broken.	91-93

Exploring Science

Exercise	Relationship to learning	Page
Chapter 2 **Body Alignment** Exercise 2 Steps 2–3	Many of the images used to present axial and locomotor movements in Chapters 2 and 3 make references to animals. Children enjoy imitating animal movements and their powers of observation are sharpened as they try to recall how an animal uses its feet, how its head and back move, and so forth. The cat in this exercise is angry, and the image can be used in the "Halloween" story in Chapter 7.	15-16
Body Alignment Exercise 3 Step 4	Coming from an overhead stretch position, the children are asked to "melt like snowmen" as they slowly come to a relaxed bent-over position.	16-17
Arms Exercise 1 Steps 1–4	As children practice arm movements they enjoy pretending to be birds or butterflies. There are differences in the ways these animals use their wings and movement provides a good opportunity to point out these *differences*.	25-26
Chapter 3 **Run–Leap** Exercise Step 4	Other animal movements can be found in the sections on Leaps, Crawling, and Creeping. Leaps, of course, resemble the movement of	31-32

Exercise	Relationship to learning	Page
	deer, tigers, and so forth. Creeping and crawling can be compared with snakes, alligators, seals, turtles, and so forth. Children should be encouraged to explain differences in these movements.	
Chapter 4 **Dynamics** Activity 2 Step 1	The movements of children on the playground can be compared with "simple machines." The seesaw is an example of lever action. Slides, ramps, and various wheel toys can illustrate ways that equipment helps people to work.	46
Step 2	The effect of a thunderstorm on the children's playing is one aspect of weather that affects us. Other weather elements such as clouds, sun, and rain can be done in movement, as discussed in themes in Chapter 7.	46
Chapter 7 **Classic Tales** Theme 1 Step 1	Jack's beans grow out of the ground and become a huge beanstalk. Children simulate the planting of the beans and the growth of the beanstalk. Discussion of how things grow and what they need to grow is appropriate. This is also relevant for the poem in the theme "The Seasons."	82
Theme 2 Steps 1–4	All of the animals in "Peter and the Wolf" behave in ways that are typical for their species. The music accompanying the actions inspires children to move like the animals they are representing.	83
Long-Term Projects Theme 1 All sections	The theme "The Seasons" is often a unit of study in grades 1 or 2. The movement suggestions can be coordinated with discussions of weather, how plants grow, the way the waves of the ocean move, and so forth. All of these topics can be enhanced through movement improvisation.	89-90
Theme 2	Movement can be developed representing animals and plants that live "Under the Sea." Much can be learned about underwater life in this project. Nothing can be more illustrative of the multitudinous forms of life and various movement qualities exhibited by them than this theme. Movement can add to the excitement of this new and different area of study.	90-91

Art Experiences

Exercise	Relationship to learning	Page
Chapter 5 **Shape** Activity 3	Awareness of shape is as important to artists as it is to dancers. Therefore, all of the activities in this section of Chapter 5 are relevant. The game of "statues" is one example of an activity that creates interesting body shapes. The children and the teacher select the best "statues" made by the children. They may compare them with sculpture, and discuss how this body shape makes them feel.	59
Chapter 5 **Level** Activities 4–5 All steps	Two children work together to create designs in space using different levels.	63-64
	Children create designs in space by forming a group of four, each on a different level.	62-64
Relating to Others Activity 4 All steps	Children plan to form a "picture," which may be abstract or may deal with some concrete idea. Groups of four perform for the rest of the class who then evaluate the "picture" and guess what it is about.	66
Floor Pattern Activity 1 Step 2	After moving on a floor pattern consisting of a figure-eight, the children make designs based on a large figure-eight, using chalk or colored crayons.	66
Activity 5 All Steps	In this activity the children create a line drawing first, and then use it as a floor pattern for movement.	68
Chapter 6 **Art-Evoked** Activities 1–4	As implied by the subheading of this chapter, all of the activities here relate to art. Colored scarves are used to interpret the feeling of different colors. Lines as floor patterns evoke various feelings. Both paintings and sculpture can be interpreted in movement, adding to their meanings for the children.	76-78
Chapter 7 **All**	All the themes discussed in this chapter can be enhanced by using art experiences as part of the project. Classic Tales can be illustrated with pictures by different children depicting various scenes of the story. Open-Ended Stories can be used to make booklets in which children	81-93

Exercise	Relationship to learning	Page
	complete the story by creating pictures that show the ending.	
	All of the Themes for Long-Term Projects can be developed into productions in which scenery, props, and costumes can be created as part of an art class. A mural for "Under the Sea" can be created as a backdrop. Children may add a fish, plants, or other creatures to the mural, thus making it a group art project.	89-92

Experiencing Music

Exercise	Relationship to learning	Page
Chapter 3 **Gallop– Slide–Skip** Exercises Step 1	The children learn to distinguish an uneven from an even rhythm. They clap the uneven rhythm of the gallop.	35
Chapter 4 **Dynamics** Activity 4 Steps 1–3	Walking in time to the drum, the children become aware of time changes, from regular walking (quarter notes) to a slow walk (half notes) to a fast tiptoe walk (eighth notes).	46-47
Accent Activities 2–3	Children learn about accent in movement and in music by taking a strong movement or by "freezing like a statue" when they hear the accented beat on a piano or cymbal.	48
Rhythmic Pattern Activity 1 Step 2	Walking and running steps are taken and the children learn to distinguish quarter and eighth notes, and to see their relationship.	49
Activity 3 All steps	Learning to do a waltz, children begin to appreciate all waltz music. They will be able to recognize the three even notes, with the accent on the first one, whenever they hear it played.	51
Activities 5–6	A percussion orchestra is basically a music experience that helps dance students as they learn to keep time, to accompany each other, and to orchestrate simple melodies.	52-53

Exercise	Relationship to learning	Page
Activity 7 All steps	Creating rhythms and orchestrating them for a percussion orchestra is a challenging task. The different qualities of the rhythm instruments is stressed. Dancers are chosen to move to the rhythm created.	53-54
Activity 8 Step 1	Beginning with the dancer's movements, the percussion orchestra accompanies him as he gives directions for each section.	54
Activity 9	Working in pairs, children accompany each other, one as the dancer and the other as the musician. They change places so that each child has both experiences.	54-55
Phrasing Activity 3 Steps 1–2	Children become aware of phrasing in music as they do different movements for each phrase.	56
Chapter 5 **Level** Activity 3 All steps	Children identify low, medium, and high sounds as played on the piano. They move on the same level as the sounds they hear.	63
Floor Pattern Activity 4	As children learn to do folk dances, they also learn the many delightful folk songs that accompany them.	67-68
Chapter 6 **Music- Evoked** Activities 1–3 All steps	All the activities in this section of Chapter 6 are relevant to music study. Activity 1 deals with the quality of sound made by various rhythm instruments. Children interpret that quality in movement. "Theme and variation" is explored in Activity 2, as the children discover that the same melody can be played in different ways and with different feelings. Interpreting musical selections in movement, as in Activity 3, is one way to heighten children's response to music.	78-80
Chapter 7 **Classic Tales** Theme 2	The classic story "Peter and the Wolf," with its musical accompaniment, is an ideal way to introduce children to the instruments in an orchestra. Moving to the various themes of the music helps children to identify them.	83
Theme 3	Humperdinck's opera *Hansel and Gretel* is excellent accompaniment for the children's enactment of the story. Familiarity with the	83-84

Exercise	Relationship to learning	Page
	music prepares them for further appreciation of opera music.	
Theme 4 All steps	Interpreting some of the scenes from Prokofiev's ballet music *Cinderella* makes the music meaningful. The children hear the ugly sisters arguing in the music. There are lovely lyrical sections for the Fairy Godmother and elegant parade music to celebrate the wedding scene. Not only the music but the ballet will be appreciated more after children have danced to parts of this beloved story.	84
Open-Ended Stories Theme 2 Step 3	The music of "Golliwogg's Cakewalk" from Debussy's *Children's Corner Suite* is fine accompaniment for the story "A Day in the Park." Other selections from Debussy's music might be chosen for listening and for movement.	87
Theme 3 All steps	Saint-Saëns' *Danse Macabre* is an appropriate selection of music for Halloween. The music has sections that sound like the characters seen at midnight in the churchyard. Children enjoy acting this out and will long remember the music.	87
Themes for Long-Term Projects Theme 2	Debussy's *La Mer* is suggested for accompaniment for the project "Under the Sea." Suitable accompaniment for any dance theme adds to the success of the project and to the enjoyment of the participants.	90-91

SELECTED REFERENCES

CHAPTER 1

Brazelton, T. Berry. *Infants and Mothers: Differences in Development.* New York: Dell, 1969.

Cherry, Clare. *Creative Movement for the Developing Child.* Palo Alto, CA: Fearon, 1968.

Fraser, Diane Lynch. *Playdancing: Discovering and Developing Creativity in Young Children.* Pennington, NJ: Princeton Book Company, Publishers, 1991.

Gesell, Arnold, et al. *The First Five Years of Life.* New York: Harper and Row, 1940.

Murray, Ruth L. *Dance in Elementary Education.* New York: Harper, 1953.

North, Marion. *Movement and Dance Education.* Plymouth, Engl.: Northcote House, 1990.

Rowen, Betty. *The Children We See: An Observational Approach to Child Study.* New York: Holt, Rinehart and Winston, 1973.

———. *Learning Through Movement.* 2d ed. New York Teachers College Press, Columbia University, 1982.

White, Burton L. *The First Three Years of Life.* Englewood Cliffs, NJ: Prentice Hall, 1975.

CHAPTERS 2 AND 3

Barlin, Anne Lief and Nurit Kalev. *Hello Toes: Movement Games for Children.*
Pennington, NJ: Princeton Book Company, Publishers, 1989.
———. *Goodnight Toes! Bedtime Stories, Lullabies and Movement Games.*
Pennington, NJ: Princeton Book Company, Publishers, 1993.
Manthrop, Beryl F. *Towards Ballet: Dance Training for the Very Young.*
Pennington, NJ: Princeton Book Company, Publishers, 1988.
Murray, Ruth L. *Dance in Elementary Education.* New York: Harper, 1953.
North, Marion. *Movement and Dance Education.* Plymouth, Engl.: Northcote
House, 1990.
Rowen, Betty. *Learning Through Movement.* 2d ed. New York: Teachers College
Press, Columbia University, 1982.
Royal Academy of Dancing. *Ballet Class.* New York: Arco, 1984.
Sutter, Beatrice and Anne Rechter. *Ballet for Children.* Waldwick, NJ: Hoctor
Dance Records, 1966.
Zukowski, Ginger and Ardie Dickson. *On the Move: A Handbook for Exploring
Creative Movement with Young Children.* Carbondale, IL: Southern Illinois
University Press, 1990.

CHAPTER 4

Cherry, Clare. *Creative Movement for the Developing Child.* Palo Alto, CA:
Fearon, 1968.
Findlay, Elsa. *Rhythm and Movement: Applications of Dalcroze Eurhythmics.*
Princeton, NJ: Summy-Birchard Music (Div. of Birch Tree Group, Ltd.),
1971.
Murray, Ruth. *Dance in Elementary Education.* New York: Harper, 1953.
Rowen, Betty. *"An Exploration of the Uses of Rhythmic Movement to Develop
Aesthetic Concepts in the Primary Grades,"* Ed.D. dissertation, Teachers
College, Columbia University, New York, 1966.
———. *Learning Through Movement.* 2d ed. New York: Teachers College Press,
Columbia University, New York, 1982.

CHAPTER 5

Diamondstein, Geraldine. *Children Dance in the Classroom.* New York:
Macmillan, 1971.
Findlay, Elsa. *Rhythm and Movement: Applications of Dalcoze Eurhythmics.*
Princeton, NJ: Summy-Birchard Music (Div. of Birch Tree Group, Ltd.), 1971.
Gerhardt, Lydia A. *Moving and Knowing: The Young Child Orients Himself in
Space.* Englewood Cliffs, NJ: Prentice Hall, 1973.
Murray, Ruth L. *Dance in Elementary Education,* New York: Harper, 1953.

Rowen, Betty. *Learning Through Movement.* 2d ed. New York: Teachers College Press, Columbia University, 1982.

Zukowski, Ginger and Ardie Dickenson. *On the Move: A Handbook for Exploring Creative Movement with Children.* Carbondale, IL: Southern Illinois University Press, 1990.

CHAPTER 6

Laban, Rudolf. *The Mastery of Movement.* London: Macdonald & Evans, 1980.

North, Marion. *Movement and Dance Education.* Plymouth, Engl.: Northcote House, 1990.

Preston-Dunlop, Valerie. *A Handbook for Modern Educational Dance.* London, Macdonald & Evans, 1963; 2nd ed. Boston: Plays, 1980.

Rowen, Betty. "An Exploration of the Uses of Rhythmic Movement to Develop Aesthetic Concepts in the Primary Grades," Ed.D. dissertation, Teachers College, Columbia University, New York, 1966.

Russell, Joan. *Creative Dance in the Primary School. London: Macdonald & Evans, 1965.*

———. *Creative Movement and Dance for Children.* London: Macdonald & Evans, 1975.

Zukowski, Ginger and Ardie Dickson. *On the Move: A Handbook for Exploring Creative Movements with Young Children.* Carbondale, IL: Southern Illinois University Press, 1990.

CHAPTER 7

Gilbert, Anne Green. *Creative Dance for All Ages: A Conceptual Approach.* Reston, VA: National Dance Association (of AAHPERD), 1992.

Joyce, Mary. *Dance Technique for Children.* Palo Alto, CA: Mayfield Publishing Company, 1984.

———. *First Steps in Teaching Creative Dance to Children*, 3rd ed. Mountain View, CA: Mayfield Publishing Company, 1994.

Lloyd, Marcia L. *Adventures in Creative Movement Activities: A Guide for Teaching.* Malaysia: Federal Publications Sdn. Bhd., 1990.

Overby, Lynnette, Richardson, Ann, et al. *Early Childhood Creative Arts: Proceedings of the International Early Childhood Creative Arts Conference.* Reston, VA: National Dance Association (of AAHPERD), 1991.

SPECIAL OFFER
More Dance Books for Children and Their Caregivers

To order, fill out the order form on the <u>next</u> page.

Hello Toes! Movement Games for Children supplies enjoyable activities for parents/caregivers and children to increase coordination and creativity. **Price: $9.95**

Hello Toes! Cassette includes Invisible Strings; Freeze & Move; Twirling; Jumping; Choo-choo; Sliding; Balloon Dance/Story; Bird in the Nest; Chay-Chay Koolay; Hello Toes; Shoo Lie Loo; Sleep Songs. **Price: $9.95**

Goodnight Toes! Bedtime Stories, Lullabies and Movement Games, the second book-and-cassette package by Anne Lief Barlin and Nurit Kalev, supplies games, methods, and activities that delight children as they relieve pent-up tensions and stretch both minds and bodies. **Price: $10.95**

Goodnight Toes! Cassette includes All the Pretty Horses; Russian Lullabye; Pajamas; Goodnight Song; Sleep Songs; Hit the Road to Dreamland; Raisins and Almonds; Goodnight Toes!; Listening Music, Classical Style; Dancing Marionette; Learning to Skip; Sprightly Rhythms; Rhythm Game; Greensleeves; Learning to Gallop; Trains and Stations. **Price: $9.95**

First Steps in Ballet by Thalia Mara, the first in a four-volume series, provides beginning ballet exercises at the barre for students age 7 and up. **Price: $6.95**

The Language of Ballet: A Dictionary by Thalia Mara is a dictionary for children ages 10 and up, with basic terms and brief biographies of legendary dancers and choreographers. **Price: $9.95**

Playdancing: Discovering and Developing Creativity in Young Children by Diane Lynch Fraser is an innovative program that develops creativity with movement, music, drawing, writing, and dramatic play exercises. **Price: $12.95**

To order, or to be added to our mailing list,
please fill out the form on the back of this page,
or call us at 1-800-220-7149.

ORDER FORM

Please send me:

QTY   TITLE/PRICE

_____   Hello Toes! Movement Games for Children/$9.95

_____   Hello Toes! Cassette/$9.95

_____   Goodnight Toes! Bedtime Stories, Lullabies, and Movement Games/$10.95

_____   Goodnight Toes! Cassette/$9.95

_____   First Steps in Ballet/$6.95

_____   The Language of Ballet: A Dictionary/$9.95

_____   Playdancing: Discovering and Developing Creativity
        in Young Children/$12.95

Name_____

Address_____

City_____ State_____ Zip_____

Day Phone_____

❑ My check or money order for $_____ is enclosed.

❑ Please charge my credit card:

    ❑ VISA   ❑ MasterCard   ❑ American Express

Account Number_____ Exp. Date_____

Signature_____

❑ Please send me your FREE dance book and video catalog.

You may phone in your order
from 8:30am–4:30pm <u>Eastern</u> time using our toll-free number
1-800-220-7149

Return this form with your payment to:
PRINCETON BOOK COMPANY, PUBLISHERS
P.O. Box 57, Pennington, New Jersey 08534